H. Harris West

# Stories from Poulan

W0006588

*Poulan Library, circa 1940's*

*Poulan Library, Present Day*

# DEDICATION

## TO THE PAST, PRESENT AND FUTURE POPULATIONS OF POULAN, GEORGIA

*Henry Hardage Home*

*McGirt's Service & Trailways Bus Station*

## ACKNOWLEDGEMENTS

I am deeply grateful to Dr. Niles Reddick for reading my stories and his necessary help with grammatical editing. Niles is an academician as well as a talented and published author of numerous literary works. I appreciate his time, interest and encouragement.

I am also indebted to my son, Guy Bryant, for his excellent photographic contributions and his organizational skills in preparing and publishing this project.

Amy Sturkey has been a valuable resource in helping my work get to the publication phase due to her first hand experience with the publishing process.

Lastly, I wish to thank my wife, Jerry, for her indulgence and patience for having to listen to my stories about Poulan repeatedly during our fifty seven years of marriage.

*Daddy watching Me Posing with Dolly and Molly on the Farm North of Doles, GA*

*My Siblings Posing with me, some First Cousins, and Aunt Mary Ethel Fambro on the Farm*

# INTRODUCTION

One of my colleagues in the Biology Department at Valdosta State remarked to me shortly after I moved to Valdosta at the end of the summer of 1968,"Harris, it doesn't take more than five minutes when you are in conversation for folks to learn that you are from Poulan, Georgia". She raised her voice in a theatrical manner as she said "Poulan, Georgia". I heartily agreed with her. I have been amused over the years with folks after learning I am from Poulan who think I am from the country Poland. I also get a kick out of their thinking that "Poolan" is the proper pronunciation. Also, I can't recall the number of times that folks believe that is the place where Poulan Chainsaws are made. I have always been a proud "Poulanite" regardless of my family's meager circumstances. They fled a share cropper's life just above Doles, Georgia around 1940 in search of a better one as employees of the Poulan Cotton Mill. I often wondered what might have been the fate of our family had it remained on the farm--but that is contrary to fact and not the way it was.

As noted in the "History of Worth County" by Lillie Martin Grubbs, Poulan was named after Judge W. A. Poulan and first settled by W. H. and J. G. McPhaul from North Carolina when they camped there on the banks of the Warrior Creek with a Negro boy around 1877. The town was incorporated some years later. My family and I entered the scene about sixty-five years subsequent to that encampment.

We used to go to Poulan weekly to see about Mama before we brought her to live with us in 2013. We would usually take a little tour of the town after visiting the beauty parlor, the doctor, or Harvey's for groceries in Sylvester. Considering the size of the town, I must emphasize the word "little". It bears some resemblance to the same place of the '40's and '50's during my "coming of age" years but the "hustle and bustle" has gone and it seems to be living in a tattered shadow of its former self. Each visit finds me frustrated as I make a futile attempt to negotiate, "what was", with the reality of "what is".

Most often when returning from Sylvester, we would take the "scenic route" and make a right turn on the old highway at what once was known as Jones's Curve opposite the site of the old drive-in theater and the Whiddon Mill Road and follow the old Highway into the west end of town. This entrance into town is presently called Northwood Drive. There were originally only two homesteads at the beginning of this point with nothing but mixed woods until reaching Mathew Webb's old service station down the hill. The station is still standing on the left but without any gas pumps or much mechanical activity taking place. Across the road is a Jim Walter style house built by Walt Gossit for his mother, sister, and himself after they moved from an old large log home closer into town. The Gossits are long gone, but the house seems to be spruced up and there is a little church nearby. I presume the house is the parsonage. Poulan has no shortages of churches no matter how humble they are. We pass the remains of Fred Carter's gum operation on the left which is not to be confused with the Turpentine Still that was located in the heart of Poulan when the industry saw better days. A noticeable horse pen has been constructed on the right just before the road begins to make a left curve. The pen and some living quarters have replaced a few old shanties where Colored folks had lived. Most all of the lovely woods have been stripped clean and you can now see the little lane that once meandered behind the property under a mysterious canopy of trees which provided another route to Warrior Creek and the railroad trestle. That little lane now is referred to as Cypress Street.

The beginning of old Poulan's heart starts at this point where the old highway turns east and leads on past the cemetery and to the overhead bridge which just about represents the eastern town limits. In today's world the old highway is known as Church Street. Nice houses bordered each side of this stretch of the highway but there were three businesses dotted within. E.P. Fletcher's little service station that was a bee hive of activity in the forties has disappeared but Mr. Frank Moore's store is now a church. Mr. McGirt's combination service and Trailways bus station is standing farther down on the left next to his house but is closed tighter than a tick.

The highway was the only paved street in town and the houses on it were a far cry better than the houses on streets where the mill folks lived, which themselves, were mostly better than the shacks that so many of the Black community occupied. As we drive along, I begin reminding my wife of the residents who lived in the houses on each side of the road as though she has never heard of them before. She is tolerant of my little ritual or perhaps she is tuning me out. I suspect she could recite family names as well as I since this exercise isn't new to her. How many times must I have mentioned the Willie Floyds, Frank Moores, Lacy Welches, Murtha Goodmans along with Sallie Jones, Merritts, Thornhills, Chapmans and Ms. Hunter. I can't forget about the Harvey Carters, Kennons, Phelps, Troutmans, Frank Kemble, Fred Davis, and Cannons. Oh, there are also the McGirts, Watsons, Hardages and Ruises before we get to the end. There have been quite a few new houses built particularly on the east end of the highway. Likewise, there have been homes erected to replace older ones burned or fallen. The little library is still a historical part of the highway and it remains in operation a few hours a week. It has a significant history and I am so glad it is still a part of the community. Ms Irene Harshburger, the Librarian during my years, would be very proud too.

Upon entering Old Poulan as we did from the east, there are about seven streets that branch off the old highway and connect one block south to Broad Street that runs the entire length of the town. This street is parallel with the old highway. It included the primary businesses but also houses to the west and east of its center. I no longer see the cotton mill which was the backbone and economic base of Poulan. The school house, the train station and railroad tracks took leave many years ago. Where is the old water tank and the little court house below where voting took place? The tiny brick jail with iron-bar windows is long gone along with the few inmates who were ever incarcerated there. "Still Carter's" house is still hanging on close by the old commissary, but what year did the turpentine still disappear? I do see Mr. Goodman's two story granitoid drug store but this historic building is on the verge of collapse and the old gas pump out front is gone. The upstairs front rooms, once occupied by Dr. Harris, no longer have window panes. Mr. Goodman is not out front chatting with Dr. Harris and Mr. Sanders, the policeman. I don't see Mr. Kennon's grocery store, but a city hall is in its place. Mrs. Hunter's old buildings and our house aren't across the street from Mr. Kennon's store. A new fire station of "Butler Building Architecture" is in that place. Mr. Alton Grays Grocery and Market is still standing but not open for business. I see no signs of activity at the little tin cafe of "third world" color, Harvey Carter's Grocery, Mrs. Jones cafe, and Webb's Restaurant. I don't see the "loafer's bench" in front of the little ice house where old men sat in good weather passing the time of day. The bank building that was previously used as a laundry mat, the post office as well as "Pricilla Garner's Studio of Voice and Music" is closed but still anchored by a marble column out front. The ancient circular concrete well in the middle of the street disappeared long ago and nobody remembers when. If we turn south in town, we travel across the old railroad bed to another populated street. It is presently known as Railroad street and turning left leads us to Pepper Street, but turning right would take us to what once was referred to as the "Quarters" where many Black families resided.

There are three streets branching to the north of the old highway that connects with the present day new highway #82. The western most street goes to "Greasy Hill" where there are some existing old mill houses along with a rather large house, which must have been the original house to the area. Folks today residing on North Elm Street probably don't know they are living on Greasy Hill. I have no idea as to how this section got its name. I do remember that the road bed was covered with numerous dark pebbles as I rode my bike and walked there. The other two streets, Hunton and Cotton, were the primary streets leading north to the Poulan School House and came together and connected behind the school at the Poulan-Shingler Road. Possum Poke was just to the right of this area. The new highway transverses this area presently.

All the streets in Poulan have names which didn't exist in my time when we got our mail by general delivery. The driving is easier now that the streets are paved and we do not have to contend with the choking dust. Passing motorists on the new #82 Highway may wonder about the significance of the sign not far from Ed's Truck Stop announcing Poulan as the "Home of Possum Poke". This was the winter residence of Governor Chase S. Osborn and still exists down "Possum Lane" but in faded glory and much needed repair. He was the Governor of Michigan in the early 1900s.

Perhaps the largest segment of the Poulan population resides in the town's cemetery. It has almost as many graves as junk cars in Futril's Junk Yard up on the new highway or about as many traffic tickets issued to motorists in that same area by the city's police force. The cemetery has witnessed considerable growth and expansion. Recently the McPhaul family gave a good amount of land adjacent to the cemetery to the city in memory of Poulan matriarch Margaret McPhaul. The land will be repurposed from growing cotton to growing graves. I have heard rumors that many out of town folks are buying burial plots there due to the lower costs when compared with other places. I do not know what effect this might have on the taxpaying citizens of the city.

I will take this opportunity to remind any readers that these few stories included in this literary undertaking are primarily from a person in his upper seventies attempting to remember "stuff" as he grew and developed from the age of two to about twenty-two in Poulan, Georgia. I solicit your kindness in overlooking inaccuracies and lack of talent that no doubt will be discovered while reading "Stories from Poulan". It might also be mentioned that many times the most interesting stories are those that remain untold.  I once read that some things might need to be left "roaming around in one's head" rather than recorded.

*Ms Sallie Jones' Home*

*An Original Cotton Mill Home on Pepper Street minus the
Front Porch*

# TABLE OF CONTENTS

*Old Downtown Water Tank*

*Present Day City Hall, former Site of Mr Kennon's Suwanee Store*

*Present Day Red Oak Baptist Church*

CHAPTER 1

# Revive Us Again

**W**hen I attended Poulan School from 1944-1952, there were nine grades. One classroom was devoted to the 1st grade, but two grades were taught in each of the other rooms. For some reason, one of the rooms wasn't used. In addition to the six classrooms, there were two office type rooms, a large auditorium, plus a boy's and a girl's bathroom. There was also a small log cabin that functioned as a lunchroom.

Beginning in the fall of 1952, it was decided that the 9th grade should be sent to Sylvester High School. I was in the first class of ninth graders to do so and was very excited about going to a larger school. There were four female teachers in Poulan School plus a male principal. One teacher taught 1st grade and the other three taught two grades each. The principal always taught the 8th and 9th grade students. I suppose the principal was expected to be smarter and more skilled at handling teen-age pupils.

I was in the 6th grade during the 1949-1950 school term and Miss Lera Hortman was my teacher. She taught all subjects except for math. Mr. Dexter Wilson, our principal, taught that. He also did some preaching in addition to his school duties. He was likable and maintained effective control of the students. Miss Hortman did a good job and involved us in different kinds of activities in and out of the classroom. She was young and unmarried with a good enough figure that could easily distract and excite pubescent males. She later married Earl Fletcher and started a family. Mr. Wilson had an extended career and became well known in both educational and religious circles. I believe that a street in Sylvester was named in his honor. He has that in common with the late Martin Luther King and other important individuals.

I suppose the ACLU wasn't too active during my school days in Poulan. We had chapel once a week with Bible readings, and each day was begun with the Pledge of Allegiance to the flag. The Lord's Prayer was standard practice. We sang songs in chapel such as "Uncle Ned" and "Old Black Joe"that would be considered racist now days.

There were five churches that served the white population during the time I lived in Poulan. On each end of Pepper Street, there was a Holiness Church or a Church of God where lots of the mill families attended. The one on the east end had a sawdust floor. This was the church that Miss Nellie Cannon attended. I remember going there one evening with Lavern Sullivan whose father and mother were real strict Holiness. On that evening Miss Nellie had brought along her husband who the town referred to as "Uncle Charlie Cannon". He loved his whisky, but he could still manage to plow a fairly straight garden row with his mule and plow. It wasn't unusual to hear him "cuss" the mule when he didn't do exactly as "Uncle Charlie" wanted. The night I was there at that church "Uncle Charlie" went to sleep and fell off the pew. He hollered "God Damn"! Miss Nellie and several others mistook his actions and thought he was calling on the Lord for salvation. They began speaking in tongues and laying their hands on him. "Uncle Charlie" finally got back on his seat.

The Holiness Church on the west end of Pepper Street looked more like a church since it had an elevated pulpit with banisters. Once I saw a preacher there do a flip over the pulpit rail and hug a hot stove. He wasn't injured because he was "filled with the Spirit". Thank God they never brought out any snakes. This is the same church that Lillian Sullivan preached a revival in one week. Lillian's family was mill workers and lived by us at one time. She taught us how to make cigarettes by rolling coffee in paper from a brown paper sack. She never attained much formal education, but they said she was ordained and "called" to preach the word of God. Several of us went to hear her one night. There was a great deal of shouting and "Praising the Lord". I recall that one teenage girl got very worked-up with Lillian's sermon. She began flopping around on the floor of the pulpit in a frenzy like a chicken that just had its neck wrung. She had a great need for repentance of her sins. She took off her rings and jewelry and threw them to the back of the church. Lots of folks, including some of my crowd, surrounded her and started "laying on of hands". Some of them had ample opportunity to "cop a feel" of various parts of her anatomy before it was over. I often wondered what happened to her jewelry.

I don't know what became of "Sister Lilian" as well as three of her siblings. Mama said her brother Lavern eventually died from asthma. All the rabbit tobacco he smoked couldn't keep him from wheezing and alive. The mother and father died sometime later. Their father, Mr. John L. Sullivan, went into the cotton mill one day and shot and killed his wife. They said he dragged her out by the hair of her head. He had a direct line with God and was only doing His will. The first shooting I recall taking place in the mill wasn't too long after World War II. Mr. Scarborough had given warning to a couple of married male employees to leave his daughters alone. They did not heed his advice but soon learned Mr. Scarborough was a man of his word. One morning, soon afterwards, he pulled out his pistol and shot the two men. He didn't kill them but they had a long convalescence.

You could count on the presence of the Holy Ghost and hearing lots of shouting and speaking in unknown tongues when you attended either of these churches on Pepper Street. This would usually take place after the preacher got cranked-up talking about Hell-fire and brimstone and you thought he wasn't going to ever take another breath. The women wore no make-up and their hair was pinned up in a ball or in a roll about the neck. Their dresses were modest with lowered hemlines and three-quarter link sleeves. Many of the women had little handkerchiefs tucked in their waistbands. For the most part, the men folk were mean as Hell during the week but got their weekly cleansing on Sundays. It was an electrifying experience seeing them get God's forgiveness over and over.

The other white churches in town were the Presbyterian, Methodist, and Baptist. The Presbyterian had very few families other than the McGirts and McPhauls. It was the prettiest church of all with stained glass windows and it sat across from the Poulan cemetery in some lovely woods. It was like "The Little Church in the Wild Wood". Even though its use was on the decline, the inside was given a big facelift for Frances Belle McGirt's wedding after she finished Georgia Teachers College. Afterwards, it sat empty for a period of time before it was torn down and replaced with A Freewill Baptist Church made out of common concrete blocks. All the trees were cut down which completely exposed the building in all its starkness to everyone that passed. The Free Will Church was begun when several members of the Baptist Church broke away and started their own church.

The Methodist Church was on Highway #82 that went east and west through the middle of Poulan. Being a highway made it the only paved street in town. This church had a sizable population and even had a little separate building in the back for Sunday School rooms. Most of the children I played with attended this church. We could always count on Mr. Murtha Goodman who was the Sunday School Superintendent to lead singing while Mrs. Elizabeth Gray played the piano. One of his favorite hymns was "In the Garden". He was the town pharmacist and owned the corner drug store. This was the largest building in town, except for the cotton mill. Mr. Frank Kemble was another regular Methodist although he would often doze-off during the service. Mr. Frank had been an organizer and officer of the cotton mill. This gave him a squire-like status in the community. He was the man mama sent me to when she needed a little loan so that we could ride the train to Macon for a weekend visit with Ma Maude and Papa English. They were mama's maternal grandparents and thus my great grandparents.

The Baptist Church was just around the corner from the Methodist Church. It was to the north and closer to the school-house. It seemed to be a larger structure than the Methodist, but it didn't have any Sunday School rooms. The church was not as popular as the Methodist and struggled for membership. This circumstance changed however in 1950 when the Baptist put on a mega revival. Mama said she believed the revival lasted for two weeks and it very well might have. Reverend Guy Carter out of Jacksonville, Florida was called upon to lead the revival, save souls, and increase membership in the church. His efforts exceeded all expectations. I never knew who was responsible for securing the services of this evangelist. Mama recently told me that he was Mr. Harvey Carter's brother. I talked with Janice Carter who is the oldest child of Harvey Carter and she said Mama was wrong. Reverend Guy Carter was the Brother-in-Law to her father Harvey. His sister was a Carter and married a Carter. Regardless, Harvey Carter was quite a prominent citizen of Poulan. He was also a Baptist even though his wife and children attended the Methodist church.

I was in the sixth grade during the time of this great revival that rocked our community. Powerful evangelistic services were held in the morning and again in the evening. I do not know whose idea it was to march the school kids down the hill to a morning church service just after the revival began. I suspect it might have been the Principal's decision since he did some Baptist preaching on the side. I know that it made lots of people mad—especially the Methodists. I cannot say for certain whether the first through the third grades attended but know for a fact that all the other grades went to hear about salvation that morning. It was a church service that affected a considerable change in the church demographics of Poulan for a long time.

Reverend Guy Carter had a stout neck. Maybe it appeared to be more so than it was due to a top shirt button that was too tight. His thinning hair wasn't enough to hide some baldness. His cheeks seemed to be a little vascular and even greater when he was "delivering the Word". He wore a suit with a vest and he bulged a little about his waist. He no doubt ate lots of fried chicken at the table of the folks that took turns feeding him during his stay. Mama was slow to come forward and be "saved" during the revival. However, she did make it in time to take her turn feeding the preacher toward the end of the revival.

The Baptist Church was pretty well full for the morning service after all the school children took their seats. I can't remember what songs were sung before the sermon or who played the piano. It was probably Tonnie Mae. She could take control of a piano like very few others. She played mostly by ear but could read music and kept a hymnal in front of her most of the time. I couldn't tell you many of the words and phrases the preacher used in his sermon that morning, but they were both convincing and convicting. He spat out the gospel like balls of fire. His words were like pictures and very real. They were like arrows shot straight from a bow. We knew those words of warning were meant just for us. I definitely didn't want to spend eternity in the hottest burning fires of Hell. A speech teacher at Georgia Southern College told our class once that a speech could be convincing in one or two ways—by EMOTION or by REASON. Reverend Guy Carter was a master at convincing sinners by SHEER EMOTION.

When the invitational hymn, "Just as I Am", was sung, the preacher didn't have to beg sinners between verses to come forward nor say at the end, "we are going to sing JUST ONE MORE VERSE to give you ONE LAST CHANCE". Patsy Smith was the first person to run to the altar. Then there was a second pupil and I was the third one to go. I can't explain how it happened, but I felt as though my body had taken flight and the next thing I knew I was up there to be "SAVED". I was shaking and my heart was beating real fast. When the last stanza was finished, there must have been about twenty-five children lined up around the altar. My brother Troy came up. He was in the fourth grade and about ten years old.

I don't remember anything about getting back up to the schoolhouse after being saved in that morning service. I believe we went straight to the little log cabin lunchroom where "Miss Irene"and "Miss Bessie" had lunch waiting for us that they had cooked on the coal stove. It might have been meatloaf, potatoes, and English peas. It could have been Irish stew with cornbread. Most of us had already been filled with "Manna from Heaven" but there was no substitute for the meals these ladies served. Whatever it was, it was both delicious and nourishing—not like lunchroom food is today or at least not like the food I had at the last "Eat with Grandparents Day".

After lunch, Principle Wilson gathered all of us that had been "SAVED " that morning and gave us a talk. Since he was a weekend preacher and the school principal it fell upon him to counsel us and explain what we had done. I don't remember much about the session, but there was some general discussion concerning the nature of sin and how to confront it. I remember on a later occasion when someone asked, "Preacher is it a sin to go to the show on Sundays?" The Palace Theater in Sylvester had begun having movies after church on Sundays. Most all of the old folks considered it a terrible sin. The preacher said, "You need to pray about this". "Go into a dark closet and ask God if it is alright". I followed his instructions that first time I wanted to go to the show on Sunday. I was fortunate that our little mill house had one closet in it. I went in to get permission form God to go to the movie. I was very relieved that he allowed me to go. I quit going into the closet soon afterward since God's answer was always of an affirmative nature. There were other more serious sins to deal with like self-pleasuring on a daily basis. Such activity might not only cause moral harm but physical damage as well. Daddy had said, "It'll make you go blind". It worried me some, but thank the Lord I have been blessed with reasonably good eyesight even though there were many un-kept promises to the Master about those sorts of things.

If we were really serious about our conversion, then there would be some expectations of how we should conduct a Christian life. If we were sure about our experiences that day, then we would have to be baptized by full immersion. Most of us were familiar with the sprinkling of water over the head that was done in the Methodist Church. Some of us had seen or heard about folks being baptized in a creek or pond. I recall that Red Oak Baptist Church near Doles had an outside cement pond with steps. Since Poulan Baptist had no baptismal behind the altar like they did in the Sylvester, it was decided that all of us who had been "saved" would be baptized at a special service at the Sylvester Baptist Church. I can't recall who the preacher was at Poulan Baptist, but he took us under the water with all our clothes on.

Reverend Carter changed many lives both young and old after that revival. Likewise new life was given to Poulan Baptist Church with so many new members. The Methodists lost most of what the Baptists gained. I don't want to imply that everything and everybody in Poulan Baptist continued in a blissful state. Two factions developed in the church about the time of our entrance. There was lots of argumentation and controversy about what direction the church should take and what kind of preacher was needed.

In 1952 when I was in the eighth grade, Poulan witnessed an even greater phenomenon than the big Baptist revival of 1950. A major tornado came through early one morning before we had gone to school. Mama and daddy had already gone to work at the mill. When I got up I noticed how still everything was outside. Not a leaf was moving and the whole atmosphere took on a greenish tint. It scared me and I hollered to Troy, "Get-up, get-up, there is something wrong". Indeed there was a great deal wrong. The tornado was around us in all its fury. I don't know how our little mill house withstood such a force. It did sound like a freight train coming. We could see all manner of objects flying. We had a basketball goal attached to a tall wooden post by the house. The tornado picked up a piece of tin and tied it in a knot around the pole. As quickly as it came, it was over. Troy and I decided we needed to get on to school. We walked to town and got us something to eat for recess at Mr. Alton's Grocery and headed up to the schoolhouse. When we reached the Baptist Church, we saw that it was no longer standing. The tornado had gone straight down the middle of the church splitting it in two. There was one big pile of splintered lumber. The tornado continued on west and took out a large stand of cedar trees and blew over numerous tombstones in the cemetery. When we got to school we learned that school had been canceled for the day. Many folks said that the Lord was sending a message to the church—and it could have been.

It took a while for the community to clean up the mess from the tornado. It took longer for members of Poulan Baptist Church to deal with having no church. The two factions that had been at odds with each other came together until a new church could be built. Several fund raisers as chicken suppers were held. By chicken suppers, I don't mean fried chicken, or BBQ chicken. I am talking about hen and dressing and everything that goes with it. It took a while but a new church was built. It lacked the charm of the old church, but it was attractive and much more functional. In the meantime funerals were held at other churches. When mama's sister Bertha Mae died, her service was held in the Methodist Church. It was a sad day no matter which church it happened to be in. After the new church was built, one of the factions pulled away and started their own church. It was the beginning of the Free Will Baptist Church.

Poulan Baptist has increased in both its membership and physical space since its new beginning in the early fifties. There have been lots of different preachers. Many were very young with great zeal and vitality that played an important role in the church's development. Jimmy Mulkey comes to my mind. He was our

preacher during my college days. He was very honest and sincere
and a great friend. He impressed me so much that I even considered going to the Baptist Seminary in Louisville after I finished
college. Needless to say, that didn't happen. Things have a way of
working out for the best.

I still keep in touch with Poulan Baptist Church through
mama. She lives directly in front of the church. In spite of severe
arthritis, she tries to attend on Sunday mornings if the weather
is good. Even when she doesn't go, she can see what is going on
through her front door. From what I gather, there is still some politics going on as usual and everyone doesn't like the preacher. Some
folks tithe and do their part and some don't. Some folks still try
to "run" the church. Some members still talk about other members. Not long ago some of the boys from a nearby juvenile home
wanted to join the church. They had been visiting regularly. Mama
bragged on them for being well dressed, good mannered, and clean.
The church decided they were welcome to visit, but they would
be denied membership. They were Black. "They have their own
church they can join if they want to," some members said.

CHAPTER 2

# A Silver Dollar Christmas

The cotton mill where mama and daddy worked in Poulan had been closed for a very long time around 1950-51 and Christmas was coming. It was evident that there would be no money for presents and all indications predicted a very bleak Christmas. Mr. Alton Gray continued to let us buy groceries at his store on credit until the mill started up again. He did this for most all of the other mill hands as well. Thanks to him we were able to eat--but not without constant worry. There were no social programs, back then, giving out aid. Families survived as best as they could. They also shared with each other vegetables they grew in their gardens. Our Thanksgiving had been meager but a memorable one. We didn't have turkey and dressing but "rooster" and dressing instead. There was only one surviving chicken from my original flock of one hundred Rhode Island Red 4-H Club chickens. The survivor was a rooster, and I sort of looked upon him as a pet as he roamed freely about the yard. As one might expect, it took a lot of courage for me to catch that rooster and help sacrifice him for our Thanksgiving meal. I always think of that rooster when I hear "She'll Be Coming Around the Mountain When She Comes" because we did "Kill the Old Red Rooster". I believe I got those chickens during the fifth grade. Daddy and Mama helped me with the brooder and later Daddy built me a small chicken yard with a chicken house made out of rough slab lumber. The 4-H Club required that I keep records of how much food I was giving them and later how many eggs were produced and sold. The assistant county agent helped me dip them for lice before the exhibition at the county fair. My chickens won a blue ribbon in the county and went on to win a red ribbon at the state fair.

On Christmas Eve that year, Mama called me into the bedroom and pulled open a drawer from the chifferobe. She unwrapped two silver dollars that had been hidden there wrapped in a purple and white silk handkerchief that was given to her by my old Great Aunt Clifford. "This is all the money we have. Papa West gave one to you and one to Troy when you all were born. I can't stand to see you have nothing for Christmas", she said. She told me to take them and go to Sylvester and buy Troy and me a present. I walked up to the highway and hitched a ride to town. I went into several stores trying to see what two dollars would buy. I finally found what I wanted for me in a shop up from the Worth County Bank and next door to the barber shop where John Edward Houston's daddy worked. It was what I called a small "scout knife". It had a beautiful bone handle and it fit into a small leather case with a loop for a belt. However, there was a small problem since the knife cost $1.25, and I was supposed to spend only a dollar on each gift. I debated about it and negotiated with my conscience for a little while before granting myself approval for buying it. I found a soccer-size red, white and blue rubber ball with stars on it for Troy and it was conveniently priced at the seventy-five cents I had left. Thank goodness there was no added sales tax in those days. I was sure Troy would like bouncing the ball as much as I would enjoy displaying my knife. I shall never forget that Mama and Papa West saved our Christmas that year.

*P.S. We played with the ball Troy got very often and it stuck around the house for a long time after the colors and air inside had almost disappeared. My beloved knife went with me in later years to Boy Scout meetings and is probably around Mama's house somewhere still.*

*Mama finally got Mr. Alton Gray paid off from the many weeks of groceries we had to buy on credit. I remember after the mill started running again Mama would give me instructions every Friday on her payday. She would say, " Take this money to Alton's and pay this week's grocery bill and pay these few dollars on our old bill". Perhaps no one was as glad as Mr. Alton Gray to see the mill running again.*

*Me in 6th Grade*

*A Surviving 3 Room MIll House Typical of the One I was Raised In*

CHAPTER 3

# Twelfth Birthday Party

**P**oulan did not have any type of organized recreational activities other than ball games played during school. There were various church activities and even a "sometimes" functional Boy Scout troop when a scoutmaster was available. Children were left pretty much on their own and besides, parents were mostly busy working and trying to make ends meet to worry about a child's leisure activities. I began working with some regularity around the age of eleven and a half. I also had to help out with home chores as many of my acquaintances did.

What I suppose I am trying to say is that I might have had too much idle time on my hands to keep my thoughts and activities out of the Devil's workshop. I don't put too much faith in that no matter how I might like to. I just have to go ahead and admit that my hormones were raging and I couldn't stop thinking about sex both night and day. I discovered that I had "matured" about a few months before my twelfth birthday and it was getting time for me to have the big experience. Listening to older boys sharing sexual fantasies and exploits only encouraged and assured me more. It was time I got some!

My first attempt was promising . There was a nice wooded area down a slight hill from the schoolhouse.  Most of the pupils who walked to school would cut through this area on a path that led up to the school.  There was a small wooden bridge over a ditch on the pathway.  On one occasion, as the area became cluttered and overgrown, it was announced that some of the higher grades would be dismissed one afternoon for a good general clean-up of the park.  It just so happened that another boy with similar sexual interests as mine was working by me in a rather obscure setting.  It also happened that there were two girls working in the same area close by.  These were the same girls who had "played around" with us in the sixth grade cloakroom.   I do not recall if it was P.W.W. or me who asked the girls for sex.  Much to our excitement the girls said, "Yes, if you can catch us you can have some!"  One could not imagine the state of our excitement as we so quickly agreed.  The next thing we knew, those girls threw off their shoes and took off like wild rabbits with us in hot pursuit.  I must mention that my friend and I were both fast runners.  In fact, I won the blue ribbon one year in the school Field Day event for the fifty- yard dash and he won it the next year.  Regardless of our speed, there was no way in God's earth that we could even get near them.  They ran out of the park on across the highway and then down town.  They turned left on the street that is now called Broad Street and flew on to the Presbyterian  church grounds and the cemetery.  They never slowed as they got back on the highway near the overhead bridge and dashed back to the school yard with two horny boys far behind.

I was getting to be almost twelve and becoming more eager for the big thing.  I had to do something that was far more assuring than going on a wild goose chase.  I made a plan that seemed quite workable for the event and proceeded to place it in operation.   January 4th was coming on and I would give myself a twelfth birthday party.  I had never had a birthday party even though I remember my sister having one in her early years.  My gosh, my birthday was so close to Christmas that hardly any mention was made of it. I certainly don't remember any presents. I could well accept the circumstance of our poverty as the primary reason. I told Mama about my plans and she agreed to the party providing it would take place on our small front porch and hoping the weather wouldn't be too cold. There was no room in our little three room house. She agreed to boil the wieners in a pot on the stove. I had very little concern for anything about the party with the exception of "how I was going to get some."

After returning to school from the Christmas holidays I began to put my plan in operation. I discussed the party with a few of the more experienced older boys who were even a couple of grades ahead of me. It was decided that my party should primarily be a "Prom Party." For those too young to remember, such a party involved games as "spin the bottle". The participants would either be all girls or all boys who would sit in a circle. The "spinner" would be of the opposite sex and spin the bottle. The person who the top of the bottle landed on had to prom with the spinner. This meant at least holding hands and walking down a somewhat darkened path. I might inject that the spinner could easily manipulate who the bottle landed on. This would be a sure bet for success in the sex department provided the right girl was there and the birthday boy was the spinner.

I could think of nothing else as the party time came closer. I had personally invited quite a number of my schoolmates to attend. Several of the boys were older by a grade or two than me. They also were looking for a good experience in the sex department. A girl who was considered "sort of my girlfriend" was among the invitees but she was in no way the object of my conquest. That role was to be played by a girl who lived close by and of more pitiful circumstance than our family. I recall that when she arrived she said, "Harris, I do not have a present". I was very gracious and said not to worry--assuming she would give me what I wanted when we got to prom. There was one big worry that I yet had to contend with. I had reached maturity and I could get a girl pregnant. I had to have some protection. One of my friends, "J", who was two years older, solved the problem. He was able to get to the Gulf Service Station in Sylvester where he had seen a "rubber" machine in the bathroom. For a quarter he was able to get a pack of three. He gave one to me, one to "R", and he kept one for himself.

It gets dark about six o'clock in January so that's about the time I told folks to come. I was so excited and eager with anticipation that I could hardly stand it. I wanted to make certain that I was fully prepared for my sexual debut. I did not want any last minute fumbling around when my prom became receptive. In order to be more efficient I went down to our outhouse and put on the rubber just before the party was to begin. That in itself was somewhat of a challenge. Mama had the wieners in the pot, the mustard, catsup and onions were on the table along with the buns and chips. The guests arrived and some even had birthday presents for me. As soon as possible, and far too quickly, I announced our spin the bottle game and the party was off. Much to my chagrin, "R" had already spun the bottle and walked off in the dark with my intended benefactor. They stayed gone a while but I was next. I got to spin and who could have guessed the bottle would land on the same girl. Off we went with my heart pounding and a very noticeable throbbing down below.

"G" and I did a marathon prom that evening. I must add that street lights were rare in Poulan back in my day. This was a perfect condition for my intended deed. I was quick to establish the nature of this walk. Her demeanor and poise was far beyond that of such a young girl. Whereas she was encouraging, she knew just what to do. We walked all over town that night. We went into Ms. Sallie Jones' Cafe where everyone could see us. We walked down to Railroad Street and passed the old cotton gin. I thought this would be the perfect place since bales of hay were stored there, but no, we walked on and on! We did the entire length of Peper

Street and on over to behind the Presbyterian Church. I even warmed my hands under my arm pits so that I might be allowed to touch her little rose bud nipples. On and on we tromped without any successful conclusion on my part. Over an hour and a half later we got back to our front porch. The porch was empty! The party was over! Mama was mad as Hell and my protective rubber was still in place!

*Poulan School, Grades 1 Through 8*

*My 4th and 5th Grade Class*

CHAPTER 4

# School Stories

## Miss Ruth

Poulan School does not enter my mind without thinking of Miss. Ruth Sumner. I address her as a "Miss" because she was a "Mrs." for only a very short period in her life. She married a farmer who had recently lost his wife. I went out to visit her in her old home place shortly before she died. She said, "Harris, I guess I should have tried to stay with that man, but I couldn't. I moved into his house when we married and it just didn't feel right. I didn't carry any of my things with me and his house was just like his deceased wife had left it. It was just like I was a visitor. I suppose I was foolish and should have moved her things out of the way, but I didn't want to hurt his feelings. This is the room I was born in and I had never known anything else," she explained as she looked around the room and back to me.

All teachers in the Poulan School taught two grades per room with the exception of the first grade. Miss Ruth taught me second and third grades as she did for years before the school closed. She had a great influence upon my development as well as with so many others. Understanding, kindness, encouragement, and patience were woven into her being. It would be a Godsend if every classroom today could have a "Miss Ruth".

I shall never forget the weekly chapel programs, plays, and fantastic year-end operettas in which she involved us. I remember the art work of pumpkins, Indians, turkeys, Santas, and Christmas trees so carefully constructed and placed in classroom windows. There has never been a smell so fragrant as the Paper White Narcissus that bloomed after being planted in pine resin cups with pebbles and water. What a great privilege it was to help construct the valentine box and later get to help pass out its contents to eager pupils. She never frowned when we gave her the Christmas gift of a little box of "Ponds" makeup more than once.

I never enjoyed an Easter egg hunt as much as those she gave us. Lemonade hasn't ever been as good since she served us that tart sweet concoction from a five gallon lard can chilled with a block of ice brought from town by trusted students. It was the perfect beverage to wash down the dyed hen's eggs along with the peanut butter and saltine crackers as we sat under the protection of a shady oak or pine tree.

Most outstanding among my memories was the safety and security I felt in her classroom. Her care and comfort surrounded me whether from a bully or two at loose on the playground at recess or some general hard times at home. Thank you Ms Ruth.

## A Foul Fowl Egg

I never remember Mrs. May Willis and her family living anywhere but in Poulan. I do recall the several different houses they lived in there during my time. Her husband died before I became acquainted with them. May was left with three sons and a daughter to raise. Bobby Gene, Randy, and Wendell were the three boys and the youngest was her daughter Garland.

May had her hands full as a single mother trying to keep afloat as most of the mill workers did. I never remember her working in the mill. She was an excellent seamstress and I believe that might have been a primary means of support. Wendell was my age and in the same grade. He was referred to as "Pee-Wee". I suppose it was because he was the male runt of their family. Everybody still calls him "Pee-Wee" even today. Bobby Gene was once mean to me and roughed-me-up one day in Mr. Kemble's garage on the way home from school. Randy was a grade ahead of me and he and I went to 4-H Camp one year together.

One year during our second or third grade, Pee-Wee decided to play a joke on Miss Ruth and the class during the annual Easter egg hunt. He was able to bring a rotten egg from Mr. Henry Hardage's chicken house to school that morning. He hid the bad egg in his desk and was going to slip it out and hide it with the good Easter eggs during the hunt. Things didn't go as planned and the egg rolled out of his desk prematurely and exploded as it hit the floor. It was the worst of smells and very unfortunate for Pee-Wee. I had never seen Miss Ruth Sumner angry before this incident. Boy was she angry! She grabbed her little paddle and lit into Pee-Wee with gusto spanking him right there with God and all her pupils looking on. Her paddle was nothing more than the bat from the "Bolo Bat" toy we all played with at the time. The bat was attached to a small rubber ball by a rubber string. The object of the game was to see how many times the player could bounce the rubber ball without it falling off the bat. The bat was the perfect shape for a paddle and it bounced off Pee-Wee's rear end quite a few times before falling off.

I do not remember what happened to Pee-Wee during the hunt and I must ask him if he was still allowed to participate after the incident. I often wonder what would have happened had he been successful with his prank. Who might have found the rotten egg? What if the finder had elected to crack it against a person's head as we very often did? Suppose that head had been mine?

### Playing Hooky

I don't remember the season as I do the year. It was during the 1949-50 school term when I was in the sixth grade with Miss

Lera Hortman as our teacher for the sixth and seventh grades. This was before she later married Earl Fletcher and became Mrs. Lera Fletcher. In spite of her youth and attractiveness, she could be quite stern when it came to classroom management.

One day as Ms Lera was calling the roll, she noticed that Bobby Gray and one of May Willis's boys were absent. I always thought it was Pee-Wee who wasn't there, but his sister, Garland, informed me it was her mild mannered brother, Randy, who had skipped class that day. Bobby Gray was in and out of my life from my earliest days in Poulan until early high school. He had an unfortunate parentage and was most often left with his sweet elderly grandparents to raise. The Grays lived just a door or two away and he was constantly around. Trouble was Bobby's middle name and there was hardly any mystery to "who did it" when he was present. The worst thing he ever did to me was physically very painful. Mama had a giant Elephant Ear plant growing in a tub on our front porch. Bobby broke off a piece of leaf and handed it to me. "Eat it. It tastes just like candy", he said. I immediately began to scream and cry because my mouth was on fire. It seemed like I cried for hours with intense burning. Mama chipped off some ice and even gave me cold milk to swish in my mouth. Nothing stopped the pain. Bobby Gray never regained my trust after that.

Our town and school were small and it was almost an impossibility for anything to be kept a secret. After Ms Hortman became aware of the absentees, Vermell Lewis spoke up quickly and said, "I know where they are Ms Lera." "Where is that?", Ms Lera replied. "They are down in the woods behind my house in a straw hut they've built", she exclaimed. Vermell lived close by the school over on Greasy Hill in one of a few cotton mill houses. There was indeed a nice large woodsy area behind her house that stretched all the way to the old highway and was abundant with pines. My brother and I, along with others, would go there, make a straw hut and spend the night. We would bring some old quilts (which would be valuable today) for bedding. We would also make a fire and cook Irish potatoes and stuff. It is easy to make a pine straw hut. All one needs is to find three or four pine trees located almost together, round up some large fallen limbs for bracing and start your hut. Use smaller limbs for support and pile the pine straw on. It's amazing how secure these huts can be.

Everything seemed to be going Pee-Wee's and Bobby's way until Miss Lera and May Willis showed up. I don't know who took over our class, but Miss Lera left and went down town to pick up May and the two them headed for the hideout. The truants were in the hut when the adults came up and demanded they come out. No matter how firm and demanding Miss Lera or May were, the response was always the same, "We aint gonna come out", they said. Becoming tired of this situation, May Willis, who was a heavy smoker, said, " to Hell with that, I'll get you out". Upon that note, she struck a match and threw it on the straw hut. As it began to catch good fire, the boys came scampering out of their sanctuary which soon became history.

## Excitement in Chemistry Class

Mrs. Mildred Warren was the Sylvester High School Science teacher during my attendance from 1952-1956. She taught me General Science, Biology, Chemistry, and Human Biology respectfully as I advanced from the ninth through the twelfth grades. She was quite an attractive lady who also coached the cheer leaders. I believe she was a Physical Education major at FSU. She no doubt had some science electives in her background in order to teach our courses of study. She was a demanding and rather good teacher. What credentials she might have lacked was compensated for by her enthusiasm and interest. She carried us on field trips to such places as Turner Air Force Base in Albany, Dixie Crystal Sugar refinery in Savannah, overnight trip to Marine Land in Florida, and a tuberculosis hospital near Tallahassee, Florida. I will always remember how our Human Biology Class was allowed to help the

County Health Department administer the first Polio Vaccinations to school children in Worth County at the VFW Club during 1955-56.

Only about eleven or twelve students were enrolled in Chemistry during our Junior year. The same classroom was used to teach all other science classes during those years. Thank God there was no Physics offered since it is too much mathematics based for me to handle. Besides the regular roes of student desks, there was a single large demonstration table in front of the room. I believe it was equipped with water and a small sink and a gas outlet for our Bunsen burner. This is where "experiments" were done. There was a stock room just off the front where all the chemicals were stored. We didn't think mercury was too harmful back then and we would pour some in our hands, roll it around, and pass it on to another.

Now that I have given you the background---here is the excitement. One day we had a big chemical explosion in class when a student mixed some dilute nitric acid with concentrated nitric acid. This is a no-no since it is like pouring water into acid. Acid should be slowly poured into water (I think). Regardless, very soon the acid shot from the big brown bottle and hit the ceiling. Acid began dripping over us and our only escape route which was the classroom door. It was also dripping over the sink area where we needed to splash water on ourselves. The teacher and students, in panic mode, jumped from a window where we were driven to the hospital close by. I must have been about the last one out the window because my green "see through nylon shirt" was falling apart. I bought that shirt from John Henry Moore at the "Empire". It must have been in style at the time and I always wore a ribbed tank undershirt beneath it. The hospital medical technologist splashed us with water. I still carry a rather noticeable scar on my right arm where the acid ate way down below the epidermis. I kept it bandaged with ointment and it took forever to heal. Incidently, the student who caused the accident went on to become a successful Pharmacist!

*Red Oak Baptist Church Graveyard, Papa (Charlie) and
Granny (Amanda) West at Red Oak Baptist Church*

*Papa and Granny's House at Red Oak, Present Day*

CHAPTER 5

# Visiting Papa and Granny West

During the early to mid-forties, my paternal grandparents Granny and Papa West lived in a small three-room house that sat directly across the road from Red Oak Baptist Church. The church is still going strong and is over one hundred and fifty years old. The church in fact owned their house. I suppose it was built as a care-taker's residence. Today the house is used as a weekend retreat for the pastor of the church. There is a large graveyard behind the church that needed to be kept in good order. No sod surrounded the grave plots as there is today. There was only white sandy soil kept hoed and raked free from weeds and grass which was Papa's job in addition to cleaning up around the church. Red Oak Church and their house were located near Doles, Georgia on a stretch of road that branches off the Ashburn and Doles Road to the east as well as the Doles and Warwick Road to the north. All the roads were unpaved back then. The eastern intersection was near Mr.

Jim Posey's house which was the closest house to Papa and Granny. The first house past the church to the north of them impressed me due to the number of lightening rods on its wood shingle roof. That was the Southwell home which is no longer standing. Mama told me Dock Southwell went to prison. "He accidentally shot and killed Cortez Houston while attempting to kill Tanny Giddens," she said. "Why"? I asked. "He believed Tanny was running around with his wife. He missed Tanny and killed Cortez instead. The bullet went right by Buford's face and he had to go to court to testify," she said. Buford was my father and all this took place at Mr. Danniel's store in Doles. "They used to drink and carry on in there," she added. On further north past the Southwell home was a little house on the left where I was born. It was near Mr. Theron Boyd's house and farm.

Papa and Granny's house had neither electricity, nor plumbing. Kerosene lamps were used at night and water was pumped from an iron hand pump out near the road. They kept a water bucket with a dipper in the kitchen for drinking and cooking. Even at a young age, I tried to drink from the dipper at a different place than I thought others had. Mama always said, "You're as 'nice-nasty' as your daddy". The front porch of the house is missing today along with the swing, but the porch roof is still there with steps underneath leading up to the front door. The door opened into the main room used as their bedroom and living room. A fireplace on the right wall was their source of heat. A bedroom to the left held two beds, and there was a kitchen to the right. A small wood-burning cook stove was in the kitchen along with a rustic table with a long wooden bench on the backside and mule-back straight chairs on the front side. A safe with screen doors was on one wall where left-over food was stored along with dishes. Like the front porch, the back porch is missing, but it once held a shelf with a wash pan and a towel hanging nearby. Papa's shaving mirror was tacked to the wall and so was his leather strap for sharpening his straight razor.

Papa and Granny were in their seventies when I visited them. They had raised four sons and three daughters. Uncle Bud (Virgil) was the oldest son and served in World War I. The other three sons were Buford (Daddy), Luther, and J.B. The oldest daughter was Aileen followed by Irene and Nora. None of Papa's and Granny's children and less than half of their twenty-two grandchildren survive in 2009. From a child's perspective, both my grand-parents looked and acted old. I will turn seventy-two soon, which was about their age when I visited them. I still remember them as "old" but don't believe I fit into that category. Hopefully, times have changed, and we truly don't look as old now in our seventies as folks did back then.

In addition to his graveyard work, Papa raised a few head of hogs in a hog pen near the woods, and Granny had chickens in a chicken yard behind the house. Papa planted a vegetable garden on each side of the house every year with peas, butterbeans, okra, and corn. In winter, he planted a crop of collards and turnips. There was no grass in the front yard-- only that same white sandy soil kept pristine from having been swept with gall berry brush-brooms. Granny used homemade broom sedge brooms for sweeping inside the house. I believe I can still make one, but it wouldn't be as tight as the brooms they made. Granny had Papa plant a double row of zinnias each year at the edge of the garden on each side of the front yard. Some Prince Feathers or Cockscombs were planted too. She had more than enough flowers for herself and would send some over to the church. The zinnias and other flowers were beautiful in the glass vase she kept in the house, but I remember how terrible the rotting stems smelled when they needed to be emptied. During the fall, she gathered the flower heads and stored them in a paper sack for seeds to be planted the following year.

Papa and Granny were resourceful people. They had to be since they had hardly any income. Papa's only money came from looking after the cemetery. Money was taken-up for his salary each first Sunday in August which coincided with Red Oak Baptist's an-nual Homecoming. I don't know if he was given all the money at once or if the church gave it to him incrementally. Mama told me that Papa and Granny had lived in two houses that burned to the ground. This might help explain why they had such meager be-longings. I still remember when I was about two years of age when they lived in a little log cabin just north of the Gleaton Place where we lived on the Doles and Warwick  Road.  I don't know much about their family lineage but sincerely doubt there was any wealth or large land ownership on either side.  Charlie West (Papa) was born in 1869.  He was one of five boys along with one sister.  He had twin brothers named Ben and Jack.  The other two were William and Jim.  His sister was named Nora.  I know nothing substantial about his parents.  Mama told me that when she married daddy they lived in the house with Papa and Granny.  She said that Papa's mother lived with them and she was an invalid.  She was more or less bedridden and Granny was kept busy looking after her.  Mama elaborated further, "Papa couldn't wait to get his hands on a little check that was sent to his mother.  He cashed it to get drunk on".  His drinking didn't surprise me since all of his sons, but one, were heavy drinkers.  This trait continues among some of his grandchildren and great grandchildren.  I am curious about the check.  I wonder if it was a pension check due to Papa's father having served in the Civil War.  The timing and age could be a supporting factor for that scenario; however, it is possible the check was some sort of welfare provision for his mother.

Amanda Smith (Granny) was from Dooly County.  I had been told she had only two brothers and a sister, but that was before checking with "ancestry. com" to learn otherwise.  I remember one brother, Uncle Willy, who lived with his and Granny's sister, Aunt Clifford.  Neither Uncle Willy nor Aunt Clifford had married.  Uncle Willy was a jolly old man that seemed to like children. He sat me in his lap once and jostled me while singing some lively ditty of a verse.  I was told Aunt Clifford could read fortunes by looking at the pattern of coffee grounds in the bottom of a cup.  It was said she foretold Granny's death on the morning before the actual news came.  I still have a silk purple handkerchief that belonged to her that was given to Mama.  I never knew Uncle Jimmy who was another of Granny's brothers.  According to Mama, he spent time in the penitentiary.  She said, "He had a machine that could make money".  I suppose it is fair to say that he was a counterfeiter.  I found out Mama was right after finding an appropriate record of his incarceration.

One of our favorite things to do while visiting Granny and Papa was to go for a ride with the mule and wagon. The last location of the mule pen was across the road out under some pines and to the right of the church. It was behind the area with long wooden tables where dinner was spread during Homecoming. Papa's wagon wasn't a wagon but a large cart since it had only two wheels. The mule was used for plowing the garden and was hitched to the cart on a weekly basis for a trip to Doles. I felt sorry for Granny since she always stayed at home. She did tell Papa once, "Charlie, don't forget my apples and graham crackers." The trip to the grocery store in Doles was no more than three miles, but it took a long time to get there and back. We followed a route that took us up to Mr. Jim Posey's house where we turned right. As we continued on to Doles, we passed Sim Slappy's house on the left. This was about the halfway mark to town. The trip gave us plenty of time to badger Papa with questions. He didn't always answer them to our satisfaction and we kept after him. I still recall the varied smells of our slow bumpy ride—the woods, the vegetation and, most of all, those smells from the mule.

Today, a portion of the route we took to Doles is no longer used as a major road and is almost obscure. I found it by going to Doles and looking to the right of a building with a sign that read Tison's Store. It is unpaved and hardly more than a single lane passage. It leads east through some fields to Sim Slappy's house where it merges with the Ashburn and Doles highway. I also discovered that the grocery store at which Papa shopped is no longer standing, but there is an open green space instead. The most striking change I noticed in my recently reconstructed trip is the complete visibility of Red Oak Cemetery and the rear of the church from the present day road. The forest that once obscured the church and graveyard is now an open field.

The long summer days spent with Granny and Papa could become a little dull. This was especially true if you were visiting alone. I recall feeling lonesome one afternoon while out by the road pumping water from the iron pump. I wished very much that someone would come. I was thrilled when I turned around and saw my double first cousin, Ferrel West, walking toward me. He caught a ride from Sylvester with Mr. Jim Posey to his house and walked on down to Granny's. He was my double first cousin since his father was Daddy's brother, Luther, and his mother was Mama's sister, Lucy Maude. Farrell was Mary Nell's age but not nearly as creative in the games department.

Most of the time we visited Papa and Granny my sister Mary Nell and I were together on these visits. She was three years older than me and equipped with a very inventive mind. We spent many afternoons out in the graveyard. Sometimes Papa would be working there, but many times we played alone among the grave plots and tombstones. Our favorite grave was one that had a marble statue of a lady. We were drawn to it and over time it seemed to become a part of us. The lady had beautiful and delicate features that made it irresistible to our constant touching. I fully believe we wore some of the marble off the statue due to our incessant clinging and fondling her over those few years. Mary Nell's imagination ran wild with stories about the marble lady and how it might represent the corpse below and how she lived and died. I found the statue on a recent visit to Red Oak. She didn't look as big as I remember and much of the surface was covered by some dark scale-like growth. It was obvious no caressing children had paid her much attention lately. We were also fond of a child's grave that had a little marble lamb on top of the tombstone. Mary Nell never ceased to construct a good story about what the child was like and how it died. The stories weren't always the same but they were satisfying and helped while-away a long afternoon out in the country.

Mary Nell scared herself, as well as me, one afternoon out in the graveyard. We were ambling by a grave when she stopped and started to carry on a conversation with the occupant below. "Mr. Greene, how are you doing today"? She asked. All of a sudden the wind started blowing bending the limbs on the large trees almost to the ground. "He's talking back to us the way dead people talk," she said as she ran climbing over the fence toward Papa and Granny's house, leaving me far behind. It scared me half to death, and I couldn't climb the fence fast enough. I fell on the other side and almost knocked myself unconscious.

There was, and still is, a good size drainage ditch behind their house. Shrubs, trees and other vegetation partially concealed an outhouse with two holes that straddled the ditch out behind the chicken yard. Over in the left corner of the toilet was a large box filled with corncobs. These were actually used for toilet paper. In Poulan, we were accustomed to using the Sears and Roebuck catalogue for that purpose; however, we always made certain we had finished our game with the catalogue before carrying it to the outhouse. My sister and I couldn't wait to get our hands on the newly arrived thick and heavy catalogue. We wanted to play "Rings and Watches". This was a game Mary Nell created. It's too bad she didn't extend this into her moneymaking ideas later in life. The rules for the "Rings and Watches" game were simple. When the new Sears Catalogue arrived, Mary Nell and I would decide which side of the catalogue was ours. It was either the left or the right. Mary Nell usually got first choice. As we turned the pages, we counted how many rings and watches were on the models. We had to skip some pages but not many. Later we included not only rings and watches, but also, all jewelry. Today would have been a field day considering all the body piercing stuff we could count. When we got to the end of the catalogue, we tallied the score. The one with the most jewelry on his side of the catalogue was the winner and got a kiss as a prize, or some promised favor. The loser got a hair-pull. Since Mary Nell was older, guess who most often got the hair-pull? One day when I reached for a cob in Papa's outhouse I saw a big snake in the box of cobs. Needless to say, I ran from the toilet as fast as my two feet would carry me. The snake was probably a rat snake and the same one, or its' kin, that Granny had seen in the chicken house.

There usually was a good crop of "outhouse tomatoes" growing in season around the toilet. We call them "cherry tomatoes" today and I will spare details of their life cycle.    Other than picking tomatoes and doing our business when nature called, we found the outhouse to be a great source of entertainment. I can't remember if it was Mary Nell or a cousin who decided we should crawl down in the ditch underneath the outhouse and watch while patrons sat on the holes above. The toilet was busy on church day and even more on Homecoming Sunday. We became so brave during our early sex education courses that we took a dog fennel, or other long twig, and tickled the rear ends of unsuspecting occupants above. We would run and hide as soon as the deed was done so that the startled folks would think it was a rampant insect or such that had paid them a visit.

On hot summer days, we often begged Papa to fill the baptismal pool, so we could swim. The large pool constructed of concrete blocks was located across the road from the church by the iron pump we used for water. It had two sets of steps. I suppose when there was a line of folks to be baptized these were used for entry and exit points. Papa never filled the pool for us no matter how much we pleaded with him. I can't imagine how long it would have taken him to hand pump enough water to even begin to fill the pool. I realize now that someone must have had an alternative means for filling the pool. The only water we ever saw in the pool was after a rain, and the water became stagnant after a while. I was a little disappointed on a recent visit when I discovered the outside baptismal pool is no longer present. I suspect an indoor pool has replaced it since Red Oak Church has undergone a great deal of change. Rather than two simple front doors with steps, there is now a front extension with a new entry. There is a large addition across the back of the church that I suspect houses a choir loft and baptismal. During the forties, there were only two doors across the back that made it look like the front of the church. I also noticed that a metal building stands to the right rear of the church. This must be the fellowship hall and Sunday school rooms. There is a lovely park and playground presently out under the pines in the place where dinner was eaten during Homecoming.

Red Oak Baptist holds its' Homecoming on the first Sunday in August. Unfortunately, this is the hottest part of the year and it coincides with gnat season. It was more unfortunate during the forties when there was no air conditioning and folks ate outside under the pines. In spite of any hardships, there was always a crowd on this special day. There would be singing in the morning and afternoon. Various folks would take turns leading the singing. Quartets and duets were also popular. The main event was eating. Each family brought enough food for themselves plus extra for guests. Mama always made Brunswick stew. She used hog's heads for the meat and added tomatoes and white cream style corn along with spices. This stew went well with the tubs full of bar-b-cue pork furnished by Mr. Theron Boyd and others. Once I remember when Mama and her sister, Aunt Lucy Maude, put several of us children under the table to eat. I was mortified when Lucy Maude handed me a fried chicken foot. When I complained, Mama threw it away and gave me a much better piece. When Homecoming festivities were over, Papa was left with some clean-up work to do. I can still remember the aroma of waxed paper "Lilly" cups that was infused with the scent of pine needles. Some "Chinet" paper plates left on the ground were fun to toss like a Frisbee. After Papa and Granny died, our family seldom went back to Homecoming at Red Oak.

On many days there was no traffic on the dirt road in front of their house, except for the mailman. Actually the mail carrier was a female by the name of Merle Tison who lived in Doles. Papa and Granny didn't get much mail. The Sylvester Local came weekly and Granny enjoyed reading "Cy Bunkus". There was a real ugly picture of him in the paper. When we were pouting or acting ugly, Granny would often remark, "You look just like "Cy Bunkus". I believe they also got the Market Bulletin. If our visit to the country was a week or more, we could count on Mama sending us a care package. It was usually a shoebox filled with a variety of sweets. I remember "Big Towns", "Kits, "Mary Janes," and a variety of other goodies that would not melt before delivery.

Sometimes we took a rest from our plundering and play and sat on the front porch in the swing with Granny. She had a supply of hand-fans that came from the church. These were indispensable during gnat season and hot weather. Some of the fans had wood handles while some others were in three sections that could be opened or closed. All of the fans had religious pictures such as Jesus with lambs and little children. Some had pictures of Angels coming out of a Heavenly sky. Funeral home advertisements were on the back of the fans. Bank's Funeral Home in Sylvester and Dekle's Funeral Home in Cordele were the primary donors.

Among my last memories of visiting Granny and Papa was when Granny was sick. She had also fallen and broken her arm. She carried it around in a sling and applied a mustard poultice to help relieve the pain and swelling. She stayed in bed a lot and couldn't put her hair up in a ball like she always did. She was a sweet and kind person, but she left us in 1946 at the age of seventy-four.

After Granny died, Papa married a niece of Granny's named Clara. She was previously married and had grown children. They lived in a little house owned by a relative of hers who lived next door in a large country home. Their houses were on the Cordele Highway about halfway between Sylvester and Cordele. I recall visiting one Sunday and eating the mid-day meal at the big house. The occasion was especially memorable due to the large round dining table with a lazy-Susan. I had never seen one. There were lots of bowls and platters of food on it, and it was intriguing to watch folks fill their plates by turning it.

Papa's second marriage was a short one since he died about two years later in 1948, one month after his seventy-ninth birthday. Mama said Clara went up to Macon to stay with one of her children after he died.

I revisited Papa and Granny recently at Red Oak Cemetery.

The tombstones that lay in the manicured lawn offer some evidence of their existence to those of us left in a living world. Although I took notice of their birth and death inscriptions, my thoughts wandered off to another place and time that was far more real to me. I saw Papa working on a hot day hoeing in the graveyard. His shirt was sweat stained and he paused to wipe his brow with the handkerchief kept in his back pocket. I saw Granny resting on the front porch in her print dress and apron. She was pining up a misplaced lock of hair. I didn't notice that the church now has a steeple or that the iron pump was no longer standing by the road. I smelled the freshness of pine boughs and heard children's sounds as they played so freely on those long days out in the country. Yes Thomas Wolfe, you can go home again. You can go home again and again, but only if you care to remember.

POULAN COTTON MILLS

*Alton Gray's Grocery, Adjacent to the Original Storage Building*
*Which is Presently the Post Office*

CHAPTER 6

# Boyhood Jobs

The first paying jobs I can remember in Poulan were picking-up pecans, picking cotton, delivering newspapers, and stacking peanuts. Later as I turned eleven years of age I began finding regular jobs working in grocery stores, delivering bread on Saturdays, working at the drive-in theater, a curb hop at Bonnie's Place and later in the Poulan cotton mill.

### Picking -Up Pecans

Gathering pecans was a seasonal job that began in the fall of the year and lasted until after Christmas. Most of the activity was around October and November. I have always said "pee-kons" but many others said "pee-cans". My pronunciation sounded better to me, perhaps, because we used a chamber pot or pee can at night since we had no indoor bathroom.

The price of picking-up pecans by the pound varied very little from year to year. Sometimes it was three cents and the highest was around five cents per pound. Sometimes we got a little extra if we climbed the tree and tried to shake the pecans down. Small boys were not too successful in shaking the trees, but Long cane poles were always good to have on hand. Most of the employers were old ladies as Ms. Merritt and Mrs. Hunter. Both of them lived on the highway. Ms. Merritt's trees were behind her house in a small grove.  Mrs. Hunter's trees were located in a grove a few blocks east of her house toward the cemetery and the overhead bridge.

I would be hard pressed to tell which of those two ladies was more difficult to deal with or which was more parsimonious. Ms. Merritt seemed more polite but would only allow us to pick up the nuts when they were completely dry; otherwise, it would not be a true pecan weight she stressed.  She gave us little buckets and sometimes coffee cans to fill.  We weighed them in a storage house and then emptied them into croaker sacks. They were stored in the same building with a variety of aromatic Watkins products which her brother, Uncle Charlie Merritt, sold.  Uncle Charlie lived in the house with her and was Governor Osborn's Chauffer when the Governor was in residence at Possum Poke.  Uncle Charlie's big black Buick was also for hire on occasion to drive folks like our family who didn't have an automobile.  I recall him driving us up to Doles a few times to visit Papa and Granny West. According to John Merritt Governor Osborn sold the car to his Uncle Charlie. As of 2015 Ms. Merritt's house is still standing but in poor shape and can hardly be seen for the junk surrounding it.

Mrs. Hunter's house was just a few doors away from Ms. Merritt's.  It was on a corner lot facing the highway and the left side bordered the beginning of Greasy Hill .  The house burned many years ago and was replaced by a more modern brick dwelling. I believe the newer house belonged to one of Harvey Carter's boys since the Carter home was next door.  Mrs. Hunter was difficult to deal with and we believed her scales weren't accurate.  She owned several pieces of property in Poulan.  The old wharf rat infested tin garage and the couple of old buildings attached to it belonged to her and were located in the middle of town across from Mr. Goodman's drug store.   Mrs. Hunter kept a cow in the pecan orchard which required us to be very careful when kneeling to pick-up the nuts.  She also had a wonderful pomegranate tree in her back yard. We never felt any guilt in liberating some of the ripe fruit when it was in season since we felt she cheated us from time to time with her pecan weighing. There is nothing that tastes quite like a ripe pomegranate and nothing I recall requires as much effort to get to its succulent goodness.

## Picking Cotton

During the mid forties, Troy and I decided to pick cotton for Mr. Russell Houston. Troy was barely of school age and I was only about three years older. We went across the road from our house to Mr. Kennon's Suwannee Store and charged two straw hats to help protect us from the hot sun. We carried along a jug of water one morning and some snacks to the cotton field that wasn't too far away. We were given some croaker bags with straps to go over our shoulders. We crawled up one row and down another dragging the sacks. It took lots of cotton to fill those bags. We felt a better sense of accomplishment by emptying partially filled bags on a large croaker sheet at the end of the field as often as we could. I can't remember how long we picked cotton that day, but in the final analysis, we didn't make enough money to pay for the straw hats we had charged at the store. I do distinctly remember the dampness on the cotton leaves made by the early morning dew, as well as the smell of the sun- warmed cotton on the sheet at the end of the field. The odor was reminiscent of our cotton mattresses after they were brought back inside from their full day of "sunning" at least once a year. All our mattresses were "sunned" during the first warm sunny days of late spring or summer. Mama said the hot sun caused the cotton in the mattresses to "fluff-up". After my Great Grandmother Ma Maud died, we inherited her feather mattress, along with her Victorian bed, dresser and wash stand. The sunning process was especially beneficial for fluffing the feathers. The beds always smelled and slept better after a good day of sun therapy. It might have been good against bed bugs, too, although I only heard about them and never saw one. The cotton picking job was very short lived, unlike the long memory of dirty knees of our overalls that held more sandspurs and beggar lice than there was cotton in our sacks and on our sheet.

## Stacking Peanuts

Peanut farmers don't stack peanuts any more, but this was standard drying practice when we were growing up. After the farmer plowed-up the peanut vines, they were "shook" to remove excess soil and then carried with pitchforks and stacked around wooden poles at strategic locations in the field. The peanut stacks were similar to the hay stacks I have seen in several old world paintings. I have missed seeing those stacks for a long time and don't remember when that part of the peanut harvesting method became extinct  The most likely reminder today of those absent peanut stacks are the large rolls of hay I see in the distant fields we rapidly pass on our way to some small or large adventure. It took more effort to stack as the pile got higher. The stacks were always much taller than small children and we were not always successful when we tried to toss the vines up to the top of the stack.

Our entire family was out at Mr. Grubb's farm working in peanuts on one occasion. The mill had shut down and all the hands were out of work. Mr. Grubb's daughter and son-in-law, Mr. and Mrs. Dukes, lived just a few doors up the street from us in a non-mill house. Mrs. Dukes worked in the mill but Mr. Dukes mainly sat around in his overalls on the front porch swing. He had a wooden leg which limited his physical activities to a certain extent. It appeared from his time spent in the front porch swing that he re-quired lots of rest. As I stated, the mill hands were out of work and folks needed to survive. Mrs. Mary Dukes asked our family if we would like to help with the peanut harvest out on her father's farm. There wouldn't be much pay, but it would be a help for those with no weekly payroll.

Troy and I, along with mama and some others, were doing the "shaking" that day, while other adults as daddy were "stacking". We were dirty and tired by 12:00 noon when the dinner bell rang.

We washed-up and went into the big kitchen where old Mrs. Grubbs had prepared a huge dinner for all the workers. She wore a turban, which I later learned, was a disguise for her baldness. The big meal in the middle of the day was almost the most unforget-table and best part of the day. The most memorable event, however, occurred when we got back to work later that afternoon in the peanut field. All of a sudden, we heard screaming and hollering and noticed Mr. Dukes running and hobbling down the field on his wooden leg. He thought he had stepped on a rattle snake. Actually, he had stepped on a bed of young rabbits. Their squeals scared him half to death. I suppose any money I made that day was given to Mama and Daddy.

The last time I remember working in peanuts is the day or two that Troy and I worked for Mr. Fouche. He owned a little farm out near Jones Curve on the Whiddon Mill Road. This was during the late 1940's and before the drive-in theater was constructed near their house and farm. Mr. Fouche paid us thirty-five cents for each stack of peanuts we made. Our wages for the day escapes me, but I do remember it took a long time and lots of pitchforks full of pea-nuts to make a stack, especially when Mr. Fouche didn't like short stacks. There is another remembrance or two about the Fouches. They had a very beautiful daughter, Grace, who was my brother's age and in the same class. She was a very lovely girl and still is to-day as I write this memory. Also, Mrs. Fouche was a Lumpkin. Her younger brother was Billy. I remember that he sent my sister Mary Nell a picture of him wrapped in a white towel. He was in the Navy and stationed in California. He also sent her a little locket with a red rose embedded in a clear plastic heart. I never knew about the relationship. I do know the picture was provocative and the neck piece was a little gaudy.

## Delivering Newspapers

The first newspaper I remember delivering was "The Grit". It was a weekly paper, in one section, and not folded as papers are today. The cost of the paper was seven cents. The carrier was expected to keep three cents and mail the other four cents from each paper to the company. There were quite a few customers in town and they most always had the seven cents to pay me. Occasionally, I would be asked to help find some of the money. I recall being told to go around back and look on the wash bench by the wash tubs and get some pennies that were left there from laundry day. As Troy and I grew older, we delivered The Atlanta Journal, The Atlanta Constitution as well as The Albany Herald at various time periods. These were daily papers and required much more work and punctuality than did delivering The Grit. The Atlanta Constitution was a morning paper and that also required getting the paper delivered before school. It was not too pleasant getting up during the dark hours of early morning to make the deliveries. This was especially true during cold weather. Often times, we had to walk since the bicycle was out of commission. Collecting was also more difficult than with the Grit. We had to do this weekly, and it was a chore to chase customers down for the money.

The worst part of a newspaper route was finding a substitute when you couldn't deliver. You were tied down. In spite of the propaganda put out by the newspaper owners that" Paper routes developed character", etc, I swore I would never allow any child of mine to have a paper route because I didn't want the responsibility of filling in for them when they couldn't do the job.

## Mr. Alton Gray's Grocery Store

At some point during the sixth grade, Mr. Alton Gray asked if I would like to help him some in his grocery store. I don't know why he asked unless he thought our family needed all the help we could get. He said he would pay me thirty-five cents an hour, and he would have to withhold social security on my wages. I got my first social security card at that time. I would report to him after school and work all day on Saturday.

My first assignment was cleaning the removable slats in the meat coolers. These were where large uncut meat was stored out of sight below the display cases. He told me to take the slats outside and wash them off under the water spigot. "You can use a meat cleaver and this wire brush to help remove the dried blood and debris from the wooden slats," he instructed. Washing those slats under cold water on a cold afternoon wasn't too much fun. I still vividly recall that very cold day and that messy chore.

I don't know why Mr. Alton thought I could drive his truck. I was underage and our family didn't even own a car. His earlier helper was an older boy by the name of Gordon Boss. Mr. Alton was disappointed when I told him I couldn't drive like Gordon had done. Obviously, I wasn't going to be very much help at the store if I couldn't do what the older boy did by making grocery deliveries. In spite of my handicap, Mr. Alton kept me on, but he drove the truck while I went along and carried the heavy boxes of groceries into the customer's homes on Pepper Street, Greasy Hill, The Highway, and other places.

There were no super markets and shopping carts for shoppers to use in the forties. Customers didn't pull their groceries from shelves nor were there any pre-cut and pre-packaged meats. Customers either asked the sales clerks for items or presented a written grocery list to them. In turn, the clerks would pull the grocery items and any meats would be cut by Mr. Alton. The groceries would be placed in cardboard boxes and paper sacks. Most of the customers held charge accounts and paid their bill on Friday at payday. Most folks bought the majority of their supplies on Friday or Saturday and charged a few daily purchases during the week. Mr. Alton Gray was a quiet and patient man who knew how to manage his money. His wife was the former Elizabeth McLendon. Her mother had taught my sister when our family lived on the Gleaton place as share croppers near Doles. She put Mary Nell up from the first grade into the second grade during her first year of school. We often heard, "Mary Nell made two grades in one year." Elizabeth Gray was the post mistress for most of my life in Poulan.

She was well educated and she and Mr. Alton had a different social life than the mill workers and most others in Poulan. They routinely attended Mardi-Gras in New Orleans many times, I heard. Mr. Alton tried to teach me a little about cutting meat. I learned how to slice bologna, spiced ham, boiled ham, and liver cheese, as well as weigh and wrap them. He gave me the task of trimming beef necks to grind for making hamburger meat. It took several weeks before I could eat hamburgers since I couldn't get the smell of beef off my hands. I once cut my finger while cleaning a knife. Mr. Alton told me how to turn the knife when I was cleaning the blade. I even learned how to cut the correct amount of cheese from the round hoop that came in a wooden box. After a while, when Mr. Alton was away, I wasn't afraid to pull out a leg of beef and cut off nice looking slices of round steak, being careful with the sharp knife and the saw used to cut through the bone.

I can't recall just how long I worked at Mr. Alton Gray's Store, but I was "let go" not long after a most embarrassing incident happened one afternoon. No one was in the store that afternoon with the exception of three female clerks and me. We were all standing around when Mr. Lamb walked into the store. He was a mill worker from Pepper Street. He was a nice looking young man with black wavy hair. When I asked him, "Can I help you"? He spoke in a low voice, "I need a box of Kotex". My face must have turned a thousand colors. What was I to do with all those female clerks watching me? The feminine necessity was well stocked and on the top shelf in direct view of everyone. In a complete state of panic, I told Mr. Lamb that we didn't have any in the store, and I would have to go next door to the storage building to get some. After grabbing a large paper bag, I took the store room key that was attached to a large wood paddle and went next door. I rummaged around the boxes but could not find one marked "Kotex". I eventually went back inside the store empty handed. All the female clerks and Mr. Lamb were waiting with all eyes on me. I told him, "I'm sorry but we are out". Mr. Lamb left the store without his intended purchase. I didn't keep my job much longer afterwards. I don't know whether it was the customer or one of the female employees who told Mr. Alton about the incident.

*P.S. My first encounter with Kotex involved Franklin Gaugh. He was a first cousin, once removed, on my daddy's side. When I was no more than six years old, Mama sent me to Mr. Goodman's Drug Store with a piece of paper upon which was written what she wanted. I encountered Franklin on the way to the store and he asked what I was going to buy. I showed him the piece of paper Mama had given me. He said, "We don't need that ", as he threw the note away and walked into the store with me. He told Mr. Goodman, " Harris' mama wants a box of Kotex". Franklin was only a year older than me and I doubt he knew much more than I did about the necessity of our purchase even though he could pronounce the word.*

### Suwannee Store

The Suwannee Store was a long rectangular building located on a corner lot diagonally across the street from Mr. Goodman's large drug store and office building. There was a front corner entrance with double doors plus a set of doors about halfway down the north side of the building that faced the street. A rear door was seldom used, but it opened onto a very large fig tree behind the store. As children, during World War II, we often played and ate figs from that tree when they were in season. Our family lived just across the street from the store and the tree. The Poulan water tank as well as the little one room court house and Mr. Steel Carter's home were also clustered behind the store.

Mr. J.W. Kennon ran the store until he turned it over to Gertrude and Russell Houston during his later years. His wife referred to him as "J.W." She talked constantly when she was in the store--hardly drawing breath between her chatter, inquiries, and suggestions. She did all the driving and I never learned why he did not drive their nice car. Mr. Kennon was always found wearing his white apron and a bottom lip full of snuff. He was a short man with a slight mid-rift bulge and a wisp of white hair combed over a balding pate. His nose was a little bulbous and slightly vascular. He very much enjoyed talking and keeping up with the happenings of the community. He did this best when his wife wasn't around robbing him of the opportunity to do so. As children, we often stopped and bought candy or some other snack for recess at school. On one such morning he asked me about my Uncle Ray Fambro, Mama's brother, who he learned had been arrested and put in jail. I knew nothing about the incident until Mama told me. Ray was Mama's youngest brother she had helped raise after their parent's death. He had been drafted in World War II and didn't appreciate it a bit. He came for a visit with us on a furlough and just decided he didn't want to be in the army any more. After spending the night with us he ended up in the Albany, Georgia jail. He needed money so he held-up a taxi cab in Albany. His weapon used in the robbery was a toy cap pistol he bought in Sylvester at the dime store. Never the less, he stayed in jail and prison for quite a long time. I recall visiting him in the Macon, Georgia jail while I was visiting at my great grandparent's home one summer.

I got a regular job at the Suwannee Store during high school after Joann Seago graduated and got married. Troy and I both helped deliver groceries on several occasions when we were children and Bill Harper wasn't available. Mr. Kennon had a little red children's wagon with side bodies that was used to deliver groceries all over town. He never invested in a truck and always used the wagon. He paid us fifteen cents a load for each delivery. Depending upon the nature of the load, pulling that wagon was often difficult considering there were no paved streets and the distance could be as far as Pepper Street or Greasy Hill. Extra care was taken when both kerosene and groceries were on board.

Bill Harper was Mr. Kennon's usual delivery man. He was already an older man when I knew him. He did other odd jobs for folks and always wore kaki long sleeved shirts and pants. In summer time his thick shirt sleeves were rolled-up, and there were very noticeable sweat marks under his arms. He wore a turned-down felt hat and he had no teeth. He rolled his own Prince Albert cigarettes and used his long tipped tongue to moisten and seal the tobacco in the thin cigarette papers. Bill walked with deliberate measured steps with shoulders and arms thrust forward with a pronounced slouch. He had a very noticeable stare during conversation due to one "funny "eye. When not working, he might be found sitting on the town loafers bench near the little ice house along with several other men. Bill Harper lived up on Greasy Hill with his elderly parents until he got married. His parents seemed normal, but we kept our distance since they were the only Jehovah's Witness people we knew. Bill surprised us when he got married. His wife was almost blind and wore very thick eyeglasses on her head of short bobbed salt and pepper hair. She was short, stout and wore turned down white socks with her black oxfords and print dresses. They lived in one of Mrs. Hunter's old half abandoned buildings across from the drug store.

Mr. Kennon had a good sense of humor and was delightful to be around most of the time. I once asked him what time it was. He pulled out his pocket watch and said, "Its half past the crack of my ass and fifteen minutes 'til farting time". I didn't find him too humorous the night he made me stay long after closing to check-up the daily receipts. We both had separate cash registers. We took in Georgia Power Payments along with grocery money. At the end of that day, I was three cents short in my cash register. He insisted on finding the three cents. I offered to chip in the three cents from my pocket. He said, "No, it is the principle of the thing." I got off much later than usual that night, and I must confess that I still cannot balance a check book.

### Delivering Bread

I worked on a bread truck beginning from about the age of twelve or slightly younger. At a younger age my family had moved from our nicer house in town into a little three room mill house down the street. Howard Seymore lived about a block up the street from me in the house now occupied by my nephew Alan west and his family. My folks knew his family. Daddy was an old fishing and drinking buddy with Howard's father-in-law Mr. Jim Corbit. They did a lot more drinking than fishing. I could never forget going with them one night up on the Flint River on a fishing trip. Thanks to God I got home safely but swore never to make such a trip again. Howard drove the Sun Beam Bread truck for Flower's Bakery from Thomasville. He began picking me up long before daylight on Saturday mornings. We would go to a storage barn in Sylvester near the Court House and load his truck with the bread that was brought earlier that morning. We delivered bread all over Worth County. I learned several valuable life lessons from this job. One of the most important was learned from delivering bread to "Sweet Lucy's Cafe". This was an African American establishment that sold, among other things, mullet fish sandwiches. There was a conspicuous sign over the cash register that read, "IF YOU AIN'T GOT NO MONEY YOU DONE ET." I didn't forget that warning and I tried to use credit wisely during my lifetime. I also never forgot the mouth-watering smell of those fried mullet fish sandwiches. Not many of the roads were paved during those days and we were blanketed with lots of dust. On hot summer days the smell of the bread and donuts mixed with the dust and fuel fumes could quickly become nauseating. There was no air conditioning and we had to drive with the windows open. Winter conditions were not quite as bad but the early morning cold was a challenge, and you kept moving to keep warm.

Howard paid me five dollars for working all day Saturday plus he bought me lunch. Most often, we ate lunch at Bonnie's Place in Sylvester. They always had a good meat and three vegetables plus bread and sweet ice tea. Howard also gave me an extra dollar if I would stay on in Sylvester until almost dark and put-up more bread when it began to give-out at Harvey's Grocery. This was the main food store in Sylvester and they sold lots of bread products. I was delighted to earn the extra money, but it meant

I had to hitchhike home late Saturday afternoon. Finding a ride wasn't usually a problem. All I had to do was walk to the north side of Austin Bank's Funeral Home on Highway #82 and stick out my thumb. A familiar car with friendly folks usually gave me a ride. There were exceptions-- but this could make for another story. Hitchhiking was a way of life for my brother and me, as well as my father. Troy and I bought our first car, a maroon 1951 Chevrolet, during the summer of 1955 before my senior year of high school. Prior to then we often missed the morning school bus to Sylvester and had to hitchhike. Daddy hitched a ride almost every afternoon after work to his favorite beer joint, the Blue Goose, in Sylvester. We quite often "depended upon the kindness of strangers" as Blanche Dubois said, as well as that of many friends with automobiles who gave us rides.

I always had a strong work ethic due to necessity I suspect. Bread trays back then were made of wood. They were heavy, and more so, when I attempted to copy my boss and carry a double load by flipping one box of bread upside down on the other. I was still a scrawny kid in spite of ordering some material from Charles Atlas. His strength building advertisements could just about always be found on the back of the "Funny Books" I read. I recall one of the ads showed a skinny guy losing his girlfriend to a muscleman on the beach who had kicked sand in his face. I regret to report that no spectacular muscles ever developed on my meager frame in spite of Mr. Charles Atlas. I suppose they were not in my gene pool.

## Drive-In Movie

In the early fifties, Mr. Moody from Omega, Georgia built a drive-in theater on the north side of Jones' Curve between Poulan and Sylvester. I believe I was in the seventh grade and was glad to get a job there after my friend Joe Hutchinson quit. I was expected to work seven nights a week and the pay was one dollar per night. My job description included meeting cars and taking money for the number of adults in the car. I brought the money to the cashier and returned any change along with the tickets. I also was expected to arrive early and get the popcorn ready along with the drinks. The worst part of the job, other than having to check the trunks for free loaders, was the bicycle trip to and from work. The trip going wasn't quite as bad as coming home alone late at night. Most of the return was a little downhill and I was able to get lots of speed as I rode swiftly through the frightening dark woods.

The drive-in job contributed a goodly amount to my sex education. As one might expect, there was ample opportunity for observing erotic activities between dating couples. I sometimes had to deliver a message from home to a patron who was supposed to be watching the movie. I recall, once or twice, delivering a message to a girl from her mother. I am a hundred percent certain she and her date were not watching the movie when I brought the message from her mama.

The drive-in job came with a few fringe benefits. I was able to eat free popcorn and coke. Sometimes eating leftover popcorn in the dark could have its hazards. In one instance I remember chomping down on a very large "June Bug". It only had to happen once before I rounded the "learning curve". I could also see the last part of the movie if I wanted to stay over after the ticket booth closed. The best movie was not always playing on the big screen but might be going on inside the projection house located rear-center of the grounds. The projectionist was the manager's husband. He had his own picture show and it wasn't "GP" rated. It was his secret that he shared with only a few. His assistant, who was about my age, told me about it and he agreed to let me watch. This was my first exposure to genuine porn movies. They were exciting, even though they were not in living color, and the actors were mostly foreign looking and straight out of the nineteen-thirties. They were much like the old French post cards but with movement.

### Bonnie's Place (Curb Hopping)

I rode south on Pope Street in Sylvester, Georgia recently to see if Bonnie's Place was still there. It wasn't. It had been replaced by a rectangular Butler-type building that appeared to be a body shop. I was not surprised that it was gone, along with so much more in my past, except from a mind that cares to remember. It would have been comforting for me to see the place again from the perspective of having worked there over fifty years ago as a curb-hop and general helper.

Bonnie's Place was a drive-in short-order restaurant located on the east end of Pope Street. This was also old Highway #82 that connected the eastern and western parts of the state. The new highway runs parallel with it but is situated a block or so to the north and today is part of the South Georgia Parkway.

Bonnie's Place, at the very least, had a "small town famous" quality about it. It no doubt began as a service station that had been transformed into the Walker family's concept of a drive-in eatery. It was a good-sized wooden structure painted white and trimmed in green if memory serves me correctly. I can't remember whether the gas pumps in front of the prominent portico were still operational by the time I came under their employ. I do have some vague recall of them. None of the parking area was paved. This made it a little messy for cars and the curb-hop during wet weather. The main interior space had originally been partitioned into more than one room. A kitchen and a storage room had been added on the back. The cash register and a long well equipped soda fountain stood at the left of the entry. There were several rotating chrome stools on the front side of the fountain. I learned to make milkshakes, malts, lemonade, banana splits and many other things at that counter. I also made simple syrup for the first time. It was a lot of sugar dissolved in water and was a common ingredient in several drinks as lemonade.

I must have begun working there at some point during the eighth grade and continued into the early part of the ninth grade. I really do not remember how much money I made per shift, but it couldn't have been much. Tips were unheard of in those days—especially since I was a far cry from a "Hooter's Girl". My first introduction to the place was when I worked for Howard Seymore on Saturdays delivering Sunbeam bread. Howard and I managed to get to Bonnie's Place around lunch almost every Saturday. They never failed to have something good to eat. It was genuine family fare with vegetables, meats, corn bread, biscuits, and tea. I am not sure how I got the job as a curb-hop. I suspect Howard told them he was about to retire and that I was a good worker in spite of my young age.

Chilidogs and cheeseburgers were the most popular food at the restaurant. I wish I had paid more attention to the ingredients that went into Vera Mae's super tasting hotdog chili. Also, you could count on their burgers and BBQ's as having been "pressed" on a warm grill before being wrapped. Too many hamburger joints today by-pass that critical step and serve their fair on a cold bun right out of the package. Hotdogs are also much better if the buns have been steamed a little before fixing them. If a steamer isn't available then a microwave can be used as a close substitute.

Bonnie's Place was named after the Walker's youngest child Bonnie. I found her to be a pleasant young woman with a vibrant personality. She was blond—perhaps by choice—and somewhat over-weight. She carried her extra pounds effectively and it became just a part of her over-all likable persona. Bonnie was no pushover and had been around enough to learn effective people management skills. Vera Mae was her older sister. She too was blond and she smoked a lot. She seemed more easy-going than the rest of the family. She was a good cook, which no doubt accounted for much of the success of the place. Vera Mae and Bonnie had some connection with Fort Walton Beach, Florida. It came up in their conversations often as they talked about taking trips down there.

Mutt Walker was their brother. I never knew what he did,

but he must have had a job elsewhere since we didn't see much of him while I worked there. Daddy Walker was a good -sized man. He was partial to wearing overalls and he loved to sit in a favorite chair while chewing on a toothpick, or maybe it was the stub of a cigar. He didn't mind giving gruff orders or making his opinion known. I was a little intimidated by him. Mrs. Walker was a gentle individual who stayed in the background. The family home was a few houses behind the restaurant and she stayed home much of the time. Unlike the business, I noticed the Walker's house was still standing on my last drive-by.

My primary working hours were in the late afternoons and at night. I always managed to find a ride to work, but they agreed to drive me home when they closed-up pretty late at night. Bonnie, Vera Mae or both, usually drove me to Poulan. I don't know why, but they always took the back road which was the Scooterville Highway. Maybe they had something stronger in their "to-go" cups than I did, and they deemed the back road a safer route for driving.

I was the only curb-hop at Bonnie's Place, and many times I could not "hop" fast enough to keep- up. There were no designated parking spaces around the restaurant nor was there any means of electronic ordering. Patrons parked anywhere they could find a place and blew their horns for service if I did not get to them shortly. Being a curb-hop required a keen eye and good sense of hearing among other characteristics. I would run out to the driver's side of the car and take the order. The order was turned-in at a window on the left front side of the building. Few folks today might remember the kind of trays the food was delivered on at these drive-in restaurants. These were rectangular metal trays that had two rubberized clamps that fit over an "almost rolled-down" car window. There was an adjustable slide-out arm on the underside of the tray that could be angled to fit the car door a little below the window and support the tray. A great deal of dexterity was required to affix the tray to the window without spilling the order on the occupants. I had a very embarrassing moment one Sunday afternoon when I spilled a bottle of Nu-Grape soda on a customer. The occupants happened to be the mayor of Sylvester, or former mayor, and his "date" Ted Phelps. I wasn't as concerned about the mayor as I was his date. Ted Phelps had been the Home Demonstration Agent in Worth County since I was in the fourth grade. She was our 4-H Club leader along with the County Agent. I had gone to 4-H Camp every summer through the eighth grade with her and County Agent Cecil Johnson. I really liked her a lot and was humiliated to spill a drink on her. I never saw much of Miss Phelps afterwards until I moved to Valdosta and began teaching at the college. A Biology student at Valdosta State, who was from Sylvester, told me she was living in Valdosta. I paid a few visits to her before she died of cancer a few years later. She never married or had children of her own, but she left a world of influence on a multitude of kids as well as many adults through Home Demonstration Clubs she helped organize.

Since I was from Poulan and not yet entered the high school there, I did not know many of the patrons of Bonnie's Place. It did not take long to remember who the regulars were. Many of the older high school students would come by only to park and buy a minimum amount. They were mainly interested in hanging out and seeing who else was there. It was annoying to have to return several times to the same car before they could make-up their minds. It was also natural that I take a little harassment from them. A normal transaction might take three trips to a car to complete—take the order, deliver the order, and return with their change. I was able to save a trip if the customer had the correct change. In fact, before I left there, I believe I started carrying some change in an apron.

### Jesse James Roberts Takes Over Bonnie's Place

At some point in 1952, the Walkers decided they wanted to take a rest from the drive-in restaurant. Bonnie's Place was turned over to Jesse James Roberts. I do not know the details as to whether he bought the place or leased it. Jesse James Roberts had a well known criminal history, but not quite as notorious as the real Jesse

James we knew about from the movies and other sources. I often wondered whether his parents intended to name him after the real Jesse James or if it were some family name. His family was from the "Bloody Ninth" District of Worth County. It got its name due to the supposedly lawless activities that took place there. We heard about a man once who walked out into a field and shot a farmer who was plowing. The victim died and the law enforcement never did anything about it. The area we call Scooterville today is located in this district. I recall going down there with my parents one Saturday night to a square dance at one of our relative's residence. They were living in a sharecropper's house out in a field. The furniture had been cleared from the front room to make space available for dancing. I imagine there was lots of moonshine and other alcoholic beverages to go along with the dancing. I enjoyed their wash pot full of boiled peanuts and the washtub filled with ice cold drinks.

I first heard about Jesse James Roberts when I read about him in the Atlanta Journal and Constitution. He headed-up a notorious car theft ring in Atlanta. He and fellow criminals had a large underground garage where they stored and worked on stolen vehicles, giving them a new identity before selling them. I don't know how long his prison sentence was or where he was housed before coming to Sylvester. I suspect due to his charming ways, and good behavior, he was eventually transferred to the Worth County Prison Farm in Isabella, Georgia. This was a minimal security facility and it was referred to as the County Work Farm.

My first meeting of Jesse was when he came to Bonnie's Place one afternoon. I assume he was there to talk about his taking over the place. I couldn't believe this tall well-dressed and well-mannered man could be a criminal. He showed us some of his leather craft as billfolds, key chains and such that he made out at the prison.

I believe Jesse began running the place during the fall of 1952. He brought two other men to help. Actually, one was just an older boy named Larry. He was a smarty-pants but fairly good looking and was always nicely dressed. I can't remember the other fellow's name, but he had a crew cut and looked mean and rough. He threw my intoxicated father out the front door of the restaurant once. Both of these characters no doubt had a criminal background. Jesse also hired a new cook to take Vera Mae's place. She was a pitiful woman who most likely had seen more prosperous times in another profession. She was as "skinny as a rail". She pulled me up close to her body one night when I was walking through the kitchen. It almost scared me to death since she was older than my mother for God's sake! I kept a safe distance from her afterwards.

It didn't take long for the demise of Bonnie's Place after Jesse James took over. The food wasn't as good and nothing was the same. The customer base quickly declined. Jesse had not really been rehabilitated, and I suspect he was using the restaurant as some sort of front for other activities. I will never forget the last night that Bonnie's Place was open.

I was making a delivery to a customer when "Smarty Pants Larry" came flying- up to the rear of the restaurant in a new- looking car. He ran into the front of the building and took all the money from the cash register. He hopped in the car and "scratched-off" with the law in hot pursuit. The car had been stolen and stored in a hay barn at Jesse's parent's farm in Scooterville. There was no one left at the restaurant but me and the cook, and the man whose name I can't remember. He told me that since I wasn't going to get paid that I could take some of the merchandise. I grabbed some chewing gum and lots of candy. He drove me home. (I don't know how the cook got home). I got up the next morning and went to school as if nothing had ever happened--but it had, Bonnie's Place had closed and I was out of a job.

*P.S. After moving to Valdosta, I read in the papers about what wonderful work Jesse James Roberts was doing as a prison counselor. I believe he wound up out in the Pacific Northwest. I want to believe he finally lived a semi-straight life before he died. If the truth be known, he probably is roaming around Heaven as a con man disguised as an angel.*

*I read in the summer 2004 issue of the "Valdosta Magazine" about when Jesse robbed the bank in Lenox, Georgia. The article gave a good description of his character and brought back memories of him and Bonnie's Place.*

*Irving Hatcher, who runs a hardware store in Sylvester and is married to the lovely Grace Fouche, told me in 2009 that Bonnie is still living. "She is somewhere down in Florida where there is lots of fishing," he said. There is lots of fishing all over Florida so I assume she could be in any number of places. He also told me that Bonnie had married a guy by the last name of Powell who was from Scooterville and that she had adopted two handicapped boys.*

*I was told that Mutt Walker, Bonnie's and Vera Mae's brother, worked at the Sylvester Local which is the weekly newspaper for the area.*

### The Cotton Mill

The Cotton Mill was central to the economic base of Poulan, and in several cases, provided jobs for more than one generation of a family. Children of mill workers could expect to find employment there as their parents and grandparents had done before them. When the mill was running-- so was the town. Likewise, when it stopped running, it brought on a small scale disaster. My first recall of it being shut down was just after World War II for a short period due to a supply and demand situation. This was the occasion when daddy found work as a carpenter. He and Mr. Griggs Thronhill helped build the cottages for the Boy Scouts at Camp Osborn. They also spent a few weeks over in Florala, Alabama helping build a peanut mill. They came home on week-ends. Daddy let me go back with him once, and let me stay with them in the hotel for a whole week. A few vivid memories linger about the hotel and the wonderful smell coming from food cooking in the kitchen. There is a very large lake in Florala that I swam in wearing a much too large navy blue wool bathing suit that belonged to some adult in the navy during the World War II. When it got wet, it weighed more than I did. It took lots of effort to swim with it and to keep it on when I dived into the lake. I also remember the afternoon about dark when daddy found me in the movie theater. He, and some other folks, had looked all over the place for me. They even thought I might have drowned in the big lake. "The movie was so good," I told him and "I was watching it for the third time." The mill shut down once again for an extended period around 1950 and the town folks suffered far more from the mill's idleness this time around.

I always hoped that I would not have to be drawn into the mill working cycle, as some of my acquaintances had, and that my future laid elsewhere. Each time I took a job at the mill, I looked upon it as a means towards an end, and it would only be temporary. I was appreciative of the opportunity that the management gave me. They also had a desire to help those who wanted to do better by staying in school. I especially liked Mr. Oron Benton who was the Superintendant when I was a junior and senior in High School. He and his wife seemed to take an interest in me--or at least, I thought they did, when I dropped in to visit them on far too many occasions. Mr. Benton was college trained in Textile Engineering at Auburn and helped me with my twelfth grade science project for Mrs. Mildred Warren's science class. I made a scrapbook with photos showing each step of how raw cotton was changed through several departments into the thread that was shipped out of the mill. The mill no longer wove the thread into cloth, as they did back during World War II. Mrs. Warren wasn't too hard to please and she gave me an A+ on the project. I must admit, it was a better project than the one I fabricated in the tenth grade where I pretended to make moonshine.

My first job at the cotton mill was clean-up work on Saturday mornings that earned me one dollar an hour. As expected, there is a tremendous amount of lint generated during the course of a week and the little cleaning made at the end of each shift wasn't nearly enough. On week-ends, the machines were shut- down which allowed for more thorough detailed grooming. There were large diameter air hoses attached at strategic locations in the mill. The air pressure in the hoses was strong and could whip the hose out of your hand if you weren't careful. All of the machines were blown-off, in and out, and underneath. The direction of the lint had to be controlled and pushed to certain collection points. It was then picked-up by hand and carried to the larger waste bin. It didn't take long for me to learn how to keep the fine lint and dust out of my nostrils. Masks were not available, but I always tied a handkerchief in triangular fashion over my nose and mouth, just as the bandits did in the western movies. Some of the workers made fun of me, but I continued wearing my protection to prevent too much cotton getting into my lungs and possibly Brown Lung Disease.

Later on I was able to get a forty hour a week job during the summer in high school as well as summer breaks in college. The minimum wage was still close to one dollar per hour, but a dollar bought a lot at the time. My primary duty was being a "creeler". Large rolls of single ply thread from the spinning department were inserted over metal rods at the top of the creel machine. Threads from different balls were pulled together and allowed to wind around a bobbin making yarn with better strength. The creeling machines were long with rows of bobbins. It took some effort to load a machine and get it started. Often, some of the threads would break, and we were taught how to lift the bobbin and tie loose ends of thread securely while the machines were still running. The filled bobbins were picked-up by another person and delivered to the winding room.

At least once a week, when the big trucks as "Carolina"

came, some of us were summoned to the loading dock for loading large boxes of yarn and very large "warps" from the warping room. We used hand trucks to load and push the heavy boxes to the truck. Bear in mind, the floors in the cotton mill were of wood construction built around 1900. There were many deep chewed-out places in the old floor. I was a feather weight back then, and when I hit one of those holes in the floor with the wheels of the hand truck, I was almost thrown over the top of the box. I did a whole lot of "cussing" when that happened just as I did when I wasn't strong enough to roll the heavy box up the ramp onto the truck. Most often, two of us were required to put the boxes in place. I especially remember such helpers as Bill Thompson and Coy Williams. I also remember those in a management position who stood around and looked on while we did the work. They talked and joked with the truck driver while we did the loading. It is somewhat the same today when I notice in public works projects that one man is doing the work while so many others are looking on.

One summer I was chosen along with a few other boys as, Joe Hutchinson, to help install pneumatic equipment underneath machinery to help curb the inhalation of lint and debris. The owners and management might have been encouraged to install this safety measure since a greater incidence of brown lung disease was being reported. We worked with a terrific guy who was brought in to handle the installation. I remember him as a charismatic mature bald man. The wages were far better than regular work, but the hours were longer and the heat was almost unbearable. Most of the installation was underneath the frames and the machines were in operation at the same time. Touching the metal of a spinning machine frame was like grabbing the handle of a hot cast iron skillet. I tried to keep working in spite of the fact I had inhaled so much lint that I had a severe sinus infection. When my sinuses began bleeding, I realized I had stayed too long on that job. I hated to quit but felt my health was of more importance than the pay.

Three shifts were in operation at the mill. First shift was from six a.m. to two p.m. This is the shift Mama and Daddy worked. Second shift was from two p.m. until ten p.m. The "graveyard shift" was from ten p.m. until six a.m. I worked once on the third shift, but I could never get used to sleeping in the daylight hours. The first shift was far too early for a teenager so my preferred choice was the second shift.

I have lots of fond memories as well as those "not so fond". I cultivated some good relationships with several of my co-workers as Mrs. Mary Dukes. She was a neighbor, who I knew from younger days, but I had grown up a bit, and we spoke on different levels during my employment. The mill had one bathroom for men and one for women. I do not know what the women's was like, but the men's was pretty terrible. There wasn't even a toilet seat on the commode and it was always filthy. I preferred our out house to that. There was a little canteen that various folks operated while I was employed. It was small and offered little choice. If I didn't bring a sandwich from home, I depended upon Webb's Cafe in Poulan to feed me. The cafe would send someone around earlier on my shift and take orders for supper. Most often it was Violet Webb, the daughter of owner Annette Webb, who took the orders and delivered the food. Her father was Matthew Webb who had been a "fixer" and a "boss" before opening a filling station and auto repair shop in town. While hamburgers were the usual, I loved the fresh ham sandwiches they made. It was made from a fresh whole boiled ham that had been chilled and sliced. It was served on fresh or toasted bread with lots of tomato, lettuce, mayonnaise, salt and black pepper. Violet later became my sister-in-law.

The mill management was thoughtful enough to build a little concrete block building with some windows for break time and smoking. It was located in front of the mill out on the lawn. One never knew what to expect upon entry. I was puzzled a time or two as to the activities going on in there since it bordered on the "hanky-panky". I was also introduced to the shower bath in the rear of the mill near the machine shop. I never knew it was there until Carlos Branch told me he was going to take a bath up there.

He lived next door to us at the time. I went along and had a bath. The best bath we had at home was during the summer when Daddy built an outside shower wrapped in tar paper with a wood slat floor and a hose with only cold water. During cold weather we bathed from a wash tub inside. There was wonderful hot water at the mill to go along with the cold. I might add, the bath and machine shop were located adjacent to the reservoir. This was a large circular pool filled with water. I suppose it was for fire protection. I do remember when it was filled with beautiful large gold fish or carp that had big fan tails. I was told that before the fish, there were baby alligators in the pool. The mill gave the gators to the park in Albany. I saw them later and they were very large specimens.

I worked a summer or two in the mill after entering Georgia Southern. Daddy had quit the mill and gone to work for Coats and Clarks in Albany in about 1957. He got mad that the management wouldn't let him have a house next door to ours that was a little larger with an inside bathroom. I applaud him for that. Since Daddy had quit the mill, our family had to move out of the little mill house. I was away in my first year of college when this took place but fortunately they moved to Banks Apartments in Sylvester. The apartment was a real treat with an indoor bathroom, which was a first for our family. Mama had to find a ride down to the mill from Sylvester and kept on working until the mill shut down for the last time. After it closed down she went to work in the Tifton Cotton Mill that was owned by the same Bud Bowen family. The Poulan Cotton Mill became a part of history around 1968 or 1969. It had been idle for some time when a fire swept over the place leaving almost as many charred ruins as memories of several generations. Presently, in its place, is a green space with some questionable plantings and a gazebo-like structure along with colorful playground equipment. Mama says it is real pretty when they put up the Christmas decorations and they have the parade.

*Former Residence of Mrs Downs and Bertha Mae on Railroad Street*

*Elroy Odom, Holding His Son, Dallas Odom, on Pepper Street*
*circa early 1940's*

CHAPTER 7

# Sitting-Up with Bertha Mae (A Snow Wake)

**B**ertha Mae died from cancer in the winter of 1952. I believe it was in February. This was a month after the big tornado had come through Poulan on January 28th creating lots of damage. Bertha Mae was one of Mama's younger sisters. She was thirty- one years old and the fifth from a total of eight children still living. Her own mother had died at the young age of thirty- five.

Bertha Mae lived a seemingly pitiful life with little opportunity for experiencing much pleasure. After her mother died in 1932, she moved with her father and four siblings from near Warwick, Georgia back up to the Barnesville and Monroe County area home place. When her father died three years later in 1935, her older brother "Tip" Fambro brought her and the other siblings back to South Georgia where he tried to take care of them as best he could. Eventually the two boys, Clarence and Ray, moved in with Mama and Daddy and Aunt Lucy Maude took Mary Ethel, the youngest sibling, to live with she and Luther. "Tip" married daddy's first cousin, Sue West, and had two children. It was very difficult during the Depression to find any sort of work. Mama said "Tip" dropped dead after walking all day looking for work. He died the year of my birth in 1938 when he was twenty-four.

Before "Tip" died, Bertha Mae married Elroy Odom. I do not know the circumstances of their meeting. My earliest recollection of Elroy was seeing an early 1940s photo of him. He was standing by his car holding their oldest child, Dallas. He appeared to be a handsome man with a wave in his hair and wore a vest with a shirt and tie. He had a big smile on his face that showed off his strong white teeth. It is my understanding from mama that a married woman other than Bertha Mae also believed him to be handsome--and even more. They would "get together"mama said when Bertha Mae was working. They didn't have to go too far to "get together" since Bertha Mae and Elroy shared a mill house on the east end of Pepper Street with that "other woman" and her husband. Each of those older mill houses could accommodate two families. Each house had a front porch with identical left and right doors that led into a two- room living space. The front room was a combination living and master bedroom. The back room was the kitchen. Sometimes an extra bed might be crammed in it as well. I suppose these houses were the precursors of what is referred to as duplexes today. Sometimes when a family was very large, the mill would allow a single family to live in the entire house. I recall that "Big-un" Carter's family had a whole house to themselves on Pepper Street. They had lots of "young-uns". "Big-un"was a logical name for him since he was a big man. He was always sitting on the front porch in his overalls when I went by on my weekly rounds delivering the Grit Paper. If it were summer time, he wore no shirt and only one strap of his overalls was usually fastened over his shoulder. The mill also might give an entire house to a single family if the man were a "fixer" or a foreman or of some other prominent rank.

Bertha Mae and Leroy lived side by side with the "other woman" and her husband in one of these Pepper Street mill houses. There was ample opportunity for a courtship, especially if found alone while their respective spouses were at work at the mill. "Bertha Mae even caught Elroy and Juanita (the other woman)'carrying on' once underneath the house," mama said. The house was raised-up, especially towards the back, by tall brick pillars. I suppose there was enough room for some amorous activity, but the entire foundation was fully exposed to the street. She must have caught them after dark I assumed. There was a double outhouse down behind each dwelling where the railroad ran pretty close up on an incline behind the toilets. I suppose there were trysting opportunities even in these outhouses. I suspect that if someone was doing any kind of business in there when the train whistle blew it might cause him or her to loose his "train of thought".

Eventually, Elroy ran off with Juanita leaving Bertha Mae and their two children, Dallas and Linda. Juanita also left her husband and their baby boy. "Her little boy was so beautiful," mama said. "I think they went down to Jacksonville, Florida". Bertha Mae and her two children moved in with Elroy's mother, Mrs. Downs. She was a Downs due to a second marriage after her first husband Mr. Odom died.

When Bertha Mae got sick from the cancer she was working at Coats and Clarks Thread Company in Albany. Mrs. Downs worked in the Poulan cotton mill on the same shift with daddy in the "creeling" room. Mrs. Downs and Bertha Mae lived on what should have been called the beginning of Pepper Street, but it was never called that. I suppose since the houses were different and not mill houses that folks didn't label it as part of Pepper Street. I don't believe that section of road ever had a name back then. Most everyone referred to Pepper Street as beginning at about the site where the Holiness Church of God sat near a curve and the road ran up a slight incline and was lined with the oldest mill houses all the way to the end.

Mrs. Down's house sat facing the tracks to the left of a narrow road that separated where white folks and black folks lived. The whites lived to the left and the blacks to the right of this little road that led south past several Negro houses and on down to the "foot-wade". The "foot-wade" was where that part of Warrior Creek narrowed and wasn't too deep. You could usually walk through it and we often did. It had an elevated plank walk over it for older folks and those who didn't want to walk through the water. This walk often got washed away during high water. The section to the right of this little road was a much longer section and was lined with several "shotgun" Negro houses and faced the train track and the rear of the cotton mill. This section was the heart of the "quarters". In reality there was just one road that was continuous but separated into three sections-- the Negro quarters, Mrs. Downs and her neighbor's houses, and that part which is referred to as Pepper Street. In today's world the first two sections are known as Railroad Street.

Poulan really didn't pay attention to street names until after I moved away. I learned a few years ago that Mama lives on the north end of Cotton Street. To my surprise, the south end of Cotton Street today is that same little road that led to the "foot-wade". The little road is much wider now and the shallow creek runs through a culvert, and the entire street is paved as is most all the others in town.

Street names and house numbers came about after the late fifties when folks started getting their mail by a postman instead of at the post office via general delivery. Some folks could afford to rent a little mailbox in the post office but not the mill hands or most others. The mail was "put-up" twice a day when the mail came in on either the dinner (noon) or evening (5:00p.m.) train. Those of us without postal boxes would stand in line until we got up to the window. The post- mistress knew our names and would look through the mail filed alphabetically. I'm certain that the postal clerk got mighty tired of us coming to check our mail. This was especially the case around Christmas and Easter when we were expecting packages that Mama had ordered from Sears.

When you lived in Poulan during my time, you might live on "Pepper Street", "Greesy Hill", "The Highway", "in Town" or in the "Negro Quarters". The former Governor of Michigan, Chase Salmon Osborn, lived in a special residence during the winter months that he named "Possum Poke". It was located at the north edge of Poulan and consisted of a two story-hunting lodge, a library, a greenhouse, and numerous other out- buildings.

Mrs. Downs's house was unpainted with a large front porch. The porch led into a large room with a coal heater and a smaller room off to the right. They used the large front room as a combination living room and bedroom. The room to the right held two double beds. There was another room off the rear of the large front room that went down to the kitchen.

Mrs. Downs could "cuss-up" a blue streak and be quite caustic to folks she didn't like. Since I appeared to be interested in her activities she took a small liking to me. She cooked me several wonderful breakfasts in her kitchen when I was staying with her for a while after Bertha Mae died. Mama said Mrs Downs might be afraid to stay by herself at night, so I should stay with her for a while until she got used to it. I suspect I was even more afraid than Mrs. Downs was, but I stayed anyway. She could also bake the most wonderful Christmas cakes. My favorite was an applesauce cake that she kept wrapped up with cloth in a box with apples and stored in a cool place until eating time. She allowed me to smell it when she periodically unwrapped it and sprinkled some wine or other spirits on it.

I don't remember when I first learned that Bertha Mae was sick and am uncertain if I even knew what cancer was. I was fourteen and in the eighth grade. I did know that Bertha Mae was having a hard time trying to work and raise Dallas and Linda. When she got sick, she got all the medical help she could from the doctors in Sylvester but continued to get worse. Somehow she was sent to Americus, Georgia to see Dr. Pendergrass. He had begun a radiation treatment program for cancer patients. I recall seeing some of the after-effects of radiation on her skin. Nothing appeared to help Bertha Mae and she continued to decline. The family was desperate. Our neighbor, Oveda Touchton, said she had heard about an old Negro man out from Lenox, Georgia who was a "Healer," and she would drive Mama and Bertha Mae over there if they wanted to go. At that point, anything was worth trying. They went soon afterwards to see if this man could perform a miracle. Mama said the man lived way back in the woods, and when they got there, he put his hands on her head and prayed or said some words. He told them they must fully believe in the "Healing Power" for it to work. I suppose they gave him some money but don't know how much. In spite of Oveda's suggestion and the "Healer's" efforts, no cure came. I might add that Oveda helped me tremendously when I had pink eye—we called it "sore eyes". This condition made your eyelids stick together in the morning with "matter" and they hurt. Oveda told me to urinate on my finger and rub it in my eye. It worked wonders! I imagined that cancer must be a little more difficult to cure than "sore eyes," but at least Oveda had tried to help Bertha Mae.

Worth County's first hospital had been recently completed when Bertha Mae finally had to be admitted. Her room was on the northeast corner of the building. Every time I carry mama by the old Sylvester Hospital she still says, "That's the room where Bertha Mae died in and I can still see her now". I too can recall the horrible experience that afternoon when I went with Mama and her brother Buddy and his wife Lorene to see her before she died. I didn't go into the room at first ,but I could hear more than I wanted to waiting outside in the hall. When I did open the door, I saw that she was being held up by Mama and them and was crying out loud and saying, "I don't want to die"! "I don't want to die"! "I don't want to leave my children". I quickly closed the door and waited. I had experienced death and funerals several times before, but I had never witnessed it so "up-close and real". I choke-up even today thinking about it.

I don't know the exact details of when Bertha Mae died. I do know that the day before her funeral was the same day that Mama's maternal grandfather, Papa English, was on his death bead. Mama and her brothers and sisters were told to hurry-up and get to Macon if they wanted to see him before he died. Mama and her siblings went through a great deal of anguish and anxiety trying to figure out what to do. Papa and "Ma Maude" had been like their own mother and father since the early death of both their parents. It was decided they must go to Macon and see Papa and try to get back the next day for Bertha Mae's funeral. There was one important detail that had to be attended to before leaving. They had to make certain that someone in the family would be available to "sit-up" with Bertha Mae's body the night before the funeral. Daddy couldn't sit all night because he had to work part of the next day and my brother Troy was too young. This left me as the sole family representative to attend the wake.

Sitting-up with the dead was a common practice during my childhood. I never recall going to a funeral home to see a body. The corpse was always brought to the house the afternoon and night before the funeral. Friends and mourners would come by at various times to pay their respects. The most popular times seemed to be before bedtime. I have heard mama say several times, "Hardly anybody was left so I had to stay all night."

The practice of holding a wake goes far back in time and it was for the purpose of watching over the dead. In earlier times, people might not have really been dead but in a coma-like condition. I doubt that this happened very often after the practice of embalming was begun. The primary ingredients for a successful wake are a corpse, plenty of food, and enough folks to sit-up that wouldn't be an embarrassment to the deceased's family. Many of my family and kinfolks who died when I was growing up were brought home. The last I remember was when daddy's brother Luther was killed. He was divorced and his family lived out of town. It was our responsibility to have the wake in our house. This was inconvenient since our little house had only three rooms—two bedrooms and a kitchen. Nevertheless, Luther and his casket were placed in Mama and Daddy's bedroom. Their bed had to be taken down first to make enough room.

I don't remember what time I arrived over at Mrs. Down's house that evening. It was well before dark. The bed had been taken down and there was a casket in its place. I can't recall the style or color, but it must have been a cheap metal one since Bertha Mae was poor like everyone else. I don't believe I have ever seen a beautiful casket no matter what it cost. They are all repugnant to me with their padded satin-like lining and fancy handles. Banks Funeral Home from Sylvester had left a supply of folding chairs along with a stand that held a little book of pages with lines for people who visited to sign their names. Several of these chairs were put around the room to supplement those that belonged to the family. There was the coal burning iron heater in front of the fireplace that was the only source of heat in the house on this cold February night. By the time I arrived friends had already brought in food that was spread around on the kitchen table. There were lots of cakes, pies, sandwich fixings, fried chicken and a pile of other things. It was more than enough for those few who "sat-up" all night.

I was the youngest among those who stayed the entire night. Most of them were women and it gave them a rare social opportunity. Since we were there to pay our respects to the deceased, the conversation centered first about her unfortunate death and circumstances. As the evening wore on towards the early dark morning hours, our chairs were drawn closer around the fire and our conversation became more intimate. Some told of bitter experiences and their general run of bad luck. Some seemed almost as bad as those of the corpse that lay nearby. As time dragged on, the talk slowed but there never was any length of silence allowed—that frightening silence where death might speak out to us and remind us of our own mortality. To help us stay awake, we would take periodic breaks and walks back to the kitchen to get something to eat; however, we never left Bertha Mae alone too long.

It was just before daylight when I kept noticing what I believed to be leaves hitting the windowpanes. This was logical since we could hear the wind blowing, but a few minutes later, it occurred to me that it couldn't be leaves since they were beginning to cover some of the panes. I looked out the front door and couldn't believe my eyes. Could that be real snow? Our hushed whispers that had formerly prevailed were changed to ecstatic cries of joy upon the realization that it was indeed snowing. We ran out into the yard not believing our eyes. In the early dark hours of the morning, there had been a renaissance that united us in a stronger bond than that of the wake inside. This was the first snow for many of us in our entire lives but death was a common occurrence. We couldn't let the snowfall go to waste and we had to leave Bertha Mae and let our friends and the entire town know that it was snowing. "It's snowing," "It's snowing," we hollered as we went through town. Some blew their car horns. We didn't believe folks would mind being awakened to see such a beautiful sight.

Dawn came on quickly and the corpse remained alone. The living was out to enjoy the snow. First daylight had exposed little drifts of white stuff that glistened everywhere. Later in the morning, we were reminded that we must leave the snow for we had a funeral to attend.

Mama and them had gotten back from Macon by that time. Papa English had not died as was predicted, but he remained very close to death. We got dressed and went to the Methodist Church for the funeral. Bertha Mae was Baptist, but the Baptist Church had been destroyed by a tornado a month earlier. We followed the hearse to the cemetery a short distance away. We anxiously watched the casket as it was lowered into a place where no snow had fallen since the grave was protected by a funeral home tent. We left the cemetery plot and looked around for the snow—but the snow, like Bertha Mae, was gone.

*The Holiness Church of God Without Spot or Wrinkle, Presently Has a New Entrance and Name*

*Shotgun Houses on West Railroad Street*

CHAPTER 8

# Memories of the Black Community

Growing-up in Poulan during the forties and fifties couldn't have been much different with respect to segregation than growing-up anywhere else in the South. My cotton mill working family was perhaps a little better off economically than the Black community--but not a whole lot better. At least, we were White, and that made a difference as for as acceptance and place. However, being mill workers was somewhat stigmatizing as is the stigma felt by many minority groups. There were those in the community with more culture, education, and class who might have "looked down on us" for who we were. The primary difference between the Negro and White citizens, other than skin color, was the historical attitude held by Whites that Blacks were considered inferior. This inferiority took root during slavery. Very few Whites realized at the time that there was indeed inferiority between the races. The Blacks were almost entirely dependent upon the Whites which placed them at the lowest economic level. Very few Blacks attended school, and when they did, these schools were much below those of the Whites. Not many folks stopped to analyze the reason for the Black condition. Not many connected opportunity and education with a better economy for that segment of the population. It might have been comforting for some poor and uneducated Whites to know there was a class of humans that perhaps ranked even below them. This prevailing attitude insured that the majority of Negroes remained at the bottom of the socio-economic scale.

The Civil Rights Movement and integration have afforded the Black population a wonderful opportunity for advancement and a better way of life. It is hoped there will be significant change, not only in economics, but in attitudes of all our citizens. However, there appears some justified fear; these many economic programs and entitlements might encourage complacency and dependency and result in a contrary intention.

The first time I heard about segregation and integration was in the fourth grade. Our teacher, Mrs. Willie Belle Watson, alerted us to some talk going on in Washington, D.C. concerning the possibility of Whites having to go to school with Negroes. I can't remember whether she spoke affirmatively or negatively on the subject, but it generated lots of thought—at least on my part. It was she who first attempted to teach us to say "Negro" rather than the "N" word that was most often used. She was married to a mill worker, but she came from a family that was more prosperous in Poulan who had seen to it that she attended college at Valdosta State. She was a good and very strict teacher, as well as was her sister, Mrs. Lillian Bius, who taught me fifth grade.

I had never given much thought about the inequity between the races. Like many others, I assumed there had always been segregation and that was the way it was supposed to be. During most of my years in Poulan, we lived in a little cotton mill house with three rooms plus an outhouse. It wasn't much better, if any, than those the Blacks lived in behind us just across the railroad tracks. Our dirt street was a little wider with much better up-keep than theirs. Many of their roads were not much more than single lanes and were in low-lying areas as were most of their houses. This resulted in terrible driving conditions during rainy weather. I recall a flood in the late forties when most of the "quarters" was under water.

Town-folks had to help evacuate many of the residents by boats. It was during that flood that my brother Troy and I were walking with daddy in very high water that was over one of the main roads that crossed Warrior Creek. We were not alone since about half the town was out to experience the marked excitement of this flooding event. We were walking barefoot when I almost cut off a toe on a piece of broken bottle. Daddy had to carry me part of the way home. It was a memorable event, not only because of the high water, but because daddy was carrying me home high up on his shoulders which was a display of caring I rarely experienced.
The main swimming hole in Poulan was referred to as the "Creek". It was nothing more than an expanded or rounded-out area of the Warrior Creek that ran through the south part of town. There were two ways to reach it. One was by a well-worn path that led from a bridge through the woods. The route most often taken was almost directly behind our house. We followed a path behind our outhouse down to the railroad tracks. We crossed over the tracks and continued on a little road past several Negro houses. Eventually, we reached the woods and then followed a turpentine trail on to the creek. Ironically, only Whites used this swimming hole even though the Black community surrounded it. Blacks fished in the creek and streams leading to and from it but did not swim there. There might have been an assumption by some that most Negroes didn't like to swim and perhaps were even afraid to try.

When I was in the sixth or seventh grade, we got news one day that two Black boys had drowned in the creek. This happened during an early afternoon and many of us left school to view the bodies. When we arrived, we noticed the bodies had been moved quite a distance from the creek bank. They were naked and were laying face-up. Being naked was not unusual, since all males swam in their "birthday suits", unless there was mixed company. The drowned victims looked more like young men to me than boys. We never heard much more about the circumstances surrounding their deaths. It was rumored that some ruffian White males might have caught them swimming in a place for "Whites Only" and could have been responsible for their drowning. I strongly suspect that wasn't the case and was indeed only a rumor.

I have encountered adults who brag a little about having grown-up with a mammy who was constantly by their side from birth. I am a little envious when I hear their tales of undying devotion to such a person from their past. Actually, I am more envious of a lifestyle that must have accompanied the affordability of having a Black Mammy. Being sharecroppers first, and working in the cotton mill later, prevented any possibility of such luxury for my family. My earliest recollection of Negroes was at about the age of two when we lived on the Gleaton Place near Doles, Georgia where my parents were sharecroppers. I remember cutting the top of my left foot. I remember some Blacks who happened to be there pulled a wad of spider webs from the porch and stuffed them in my wound to help stop the bleeding.

After moving to Poulan, I recall a few Blacks that my folks employed to keep an eye on us when we were very young and they were at work. Once we attained grade school level, we were left by ourselves. The first person I remember keeping us was Verna. She drank a lot and was soon found to be undependable. There was a young girl after Verna who stayed with us a few times. I remember her cutting out women from the underwear section of the Sears and Roebuck catalogue and playing "games" with us. I am sure mama would love to have known about that while she was working.

During the later forties, the Negroes living closest to us were "Nig" and his wife Pearlene. I do not know their last names. Pearlene was one of the daughters of Rena Mae Billingsly. Rena Mae was an Amazon of a woman with thick lips and huge feet. She was stronger than many men I knew. She owned her own neat little house on the road that we took to the creek. It was a few houses down from Nig and Pearlene. She worked very hard at all kinds of jobs and raised several children. The last job I remember her doing was picking up trash and garbage for the city. Pearlene and

"Nig" lived just across the railroad track from us and they had several children. We used to play with one of their sons who we called "Noodie". I don't know if that was his real name. We often would dig foxholes and cover them with straw or other material. These were our hideouts. One of our favorites was in the broom sedge field near the railroad tracks and near Noodie's house. Many afternoons we would have an Irish potato fry at the foxhole. Someone would bring potatoes while others brought grease or a frying pan. The potatoes were always sliced thin and round like real potato chips. They were delicious and hardly got done and out of the pan before they were eaten. The potatoes were cooked over a fire built between some bricks. Once, we became a little careless on a windy day and the fire got out of control. Since the foxhole was in the middle of a broom sedge field the fire spread rapidly. It threatened some outhouses and even the crossties on the railroad near Noodie's house. It's no telling what might have happened had mama not come to our rescue. I don't know what became of Noodie, but I believe Pearlene left Nig and moved up North. Nig might not have been the most faithful husband, but he could be counted on to beat the drums at church on weekends.

While there were several Negro churches in Poulan, one stands out in memory. It was a simple wooden structure just across the tracks on the road that led out to the Scooterville Road. There was a sign over the front entrance that read, "The Holiness Church of God Without Spot or Wrinkle". The sign was no more than a board with the crudely written words inscribed on it with white paint. This church is still standing today but has another name. The most unusual thing about the church was the sound of beating drums that began coming from it about nightfall on Friday and continued until Sunday night. It was a rather deep base sound and seemed to be coming straight out of Africa. Nig was one of the men who beat the drum. I never saw it, but someone said the drum was a piece of rubber stretched over a washtub.

When I was at Georgia Southern, during my senior year, I

took a music appreciation course. I never knew much about music while growing up. We listened to the "Grand Old Opry" on Saturday nights. When I was in high school, I took voice lessons from Mrs. Pricilla Garner in Poulan. Her studio, as well as her residence, was in the old bank building which had been used previously as the post office. I took group lessons for fifty cents a lesson. Later, I was able to manage some individual instruction. I sang a couple of times on the Albany T.V. station. The program was "Home with the Hulicks" and it aired at 2:00p.m. Once Mr. Hulick asked me on the air what my vocal range was. I didn't know what he was talking about. I was frequently called upon to sing at weddings in town since there wasn't anybody else to ask. I also led singing at Poulan Baptist Church and did a few solos.

My instructor for the Music Appreciation class at Georgia Southern was a Miss Thomas from Michigan. She was just out of graduate school and was a young and striking woman. The hemline of her apparel was always just above her knee and she wore high heels. She started off the course by having us listen to "Country and Western" music. She must have assumed it was preferential for our geographic region. It wasn't long before we got into the higher-class stuff like rondos and fugues. Miss Thomas informed our class that there were two things indigenous to the United States. One was the "Wild West" and the other was the "Negro Spiritual". When it came time for writing my term paper, I chose to do it on the "Negro Spiritual". I did a little library work but added a lot about my personal experience and observations at "The Holiness Church of God Without Spot or Wrinkle" in Poulan. I did manage to go down near the church and sit on the railroad tracks one night and listen. Some folks thought I was crazy, or drunk, but I called it doing research. I made an "A" on the paper. I needed the grade since I found it difficult to identify "what movement?" from "what composition?" when she placed the needle on a recording and quickly removed it on test day. I doubt the drum beating is still going on at that church today since there most probably is a noise level ordinance in Poulan by now.

Some of the Negro women in Poulan took in washing and ironing. They used a wash pot, washtubs, and a rub board for washing clothes and used flat irons heated on a stove for ironing. This was no different from our house since Mama usually did our laundry most of the time using the same methods. There were a few instances when we sent our clothes out to be washed, but that was a rarity.

In the early fifties, Mama bought our first washing machine. The wringer was at the top and consisted of two rollers into which the wet clothes were fed. Our machine was on the back porch and we filled it with water from a piece of garden hose that we attached to the outside spigot. After the clothes finished washing, they were run through the wringers into a tub of rinse water. When Mama first started using the machine, she got one of her hands caught in the ringer. She was so flustered that her entire arm, up to her elbow, went through the wringer before she could remember how to disengage the rollers. She still complains today about her arm hurting as a result of that mishap long ago.

Mary Robinson and "Aunt Sally" come to mind as helping us some with our laundry. Mary Robinson was a sweet person and seemed to like children. Her skin was blotched on her hands and arms. I felt sorry for her since I thought she must have done too much washing with bleach. Once Shirley Fredrick and her sister, Ann, along with Mary Nell and I were playing under the bridge that went over Warrior Creek. We got wet due to our sloshing around in the water. We became worried about what our mamas would say. It wasn't summer time and we were cold. Mary Robinson let us into her house to get warm and dry our clothes by her wood burning stove before going home.

Out of respect, children often referred to older Negroes as "Aunt" or "Uncle". No one knew how old she was, but "Aunt Sally" was a fixture in Poulan long before I was born. She was extremely bow-legged, so much so, we often wondered how she was able to walk. In her earlier years, she also took-in washing and ironing. She knew many children's parents when they were children. We always enjoyed talking and visiting with her.

There was an elderly man about the equivalent in age to Aunt Sally. We knew him as "Uncle Henry". He lived a good distance down the railroad tracks in an isolated house near the trestle that ran over Warrior Creek. I delivered the Grit Paper to him each week. He had beautiful white hair and beard. He looked exactly like Uncle Remus from the movie "Song of the South". It was somewhat adventurous to take the opportunity to look around his house while he tried to find seven cents to pay for the paper.

No Negro male stands out more in my childhood memory than Clem. He worked in the turpentine business. I never saw him without his knee-high rubber boots as well as his cap. He drove an unusual wagon that was equipped with automobile tires rather than standard wagon wheels. This made it easier to haul the barrels of gum from the woods to the turpentine still in town. The largest horses we had ever seen pulled his wagon. I believe someone said the horses came from Belgium. They had really big feet.

The naval store's business was not nearly as booming during the forties as it had once been. There were not too many men who chipped pine trees and later came around to empty the gum that had collected in metal cups attached below the chipped area. Clem was one of the last to live this way of life. In earlier times, not only was there a turpentine still in Poulan, but also a commissary where workers bought their goods. This was a company store and was located near the owner's or overseer's home. This store was similar to the commissaries that once operated on large farms throughout the south and supplied the many sharecroppers with food and other goods.

The turpentine still was where turpentine was derived from crude gum or resin from pine trees. The crude gum was heated in a large vat and the vapor was distilled and collected as spirits of turpentine. The residual matter was drained off at the bottom and was converted into rosin that was marketed for several uses. Mama always kept a bottle of turpentine in the house for medicinal purposes. It was good to pour over a cut wound. It was also standard practice at our house to take a spoonful of sugar with few drops of turpentine on it to help with the "croup". It was also good when mixed with hot tallow and applied to the chest.

The turpentine still in Poulan was quite close to the front of a house we lived in during the early forties. The still was behind the water tank and the one-room courthouse. It is no longer standing today; however, the commissary remains next to "Still Carter's" house. "Still Carter" was an early owner or overseer of the turpentine operation in Poulan.

Inside the turpentine still was a plank catwalk that went all the way around the vat. The walk was narrow and high up off the ground just below the top of the vat. The workers could observe the cooking process and allow them to walk around and skim off any floating debris that might rise to the top. One of our favorite places to explore and play was around the turpentine still. While exciting, it was not the safest playground. We would run around the catwalk being careful not to fall into the vat of hot spirits. We might even pretend that we were going to push someone in. We had to keep a watchful eye for Clem since he would run us off. "You 'young-uns' better stay away from that vat lest you be like that little boy who fell in there", he said. "All that was left of him was his bones cause his skin just melted off", he continued. We only halfway believed him since we kept going back only to be run off again.

Ethel Rhymes was one of the Negro women who worked at "Possum Poke" which was the winter residence of the ex-governor of Michigan Chase S. Osborn. After the Governor died, she remained with his widow Stellanova. Ethel was always at the residence when Stellanova was there and often times when she wasn't.

As a teenager, I frequently sought refuge and solitude out at Possum Poke. If Ethel was there, we would have some good conversation and she left me alone to walk around the place. She did the cooking as well as other chores as others had done before her. In my childhood days, I recall her tending to the turkeys and chickens. When Stellanova was away, Ethel worked for other folks in town. She had her own house on the little road that led to the foot-wade. Ethel loved to laugh and caused others to laugh with her. She was a joyful person and that is why she was a favorite among those who came in contact with her. I can still see her vividly now as well as hear her voice as she rolled her hands in her white apron.

One of the nicest Negro families with which I was acquainted in Poulan was the George Jones family. When they came to the Suwannee store for groceries, they were always well-dressed and used perfect manners. Mr. Jones might have been a preacher or teacher. His level of education and his general demeanor was far above most of the Blacks, as well as the Whites, who came into the store. His daughters wore pigtails with bows and they were very well behaved and pretty. George and his family lived in one of the most beautiful locations in Poulan. Their house was on a little dirt road framed by a canopy of trees. The road branched off old Highway 82 at the west end of town and went through some woods before merging again with the highway. I drove by their house recently during late winter. The yard was filled with blooming Narcissus. I picked a few in sweet memory of Miss Ruth Sumner who was my second and third grade teacher. The house had been changed a bit and, of course, the Jones family had left long ago.

My remembrances of the Poulan Negro Community would be incomplete without including Plentis Dupree. Plentis was a small slim man who was real popular in the community. He might have been more popular among those who wished to buy moonshine. He was the man I was referred to when I needed to buy a little "shine" for my eleventh grade science project. I coasted along all year knowing I had to have a science project for Mrs. Warren's chemistry class. Just before it was due, I had to create something fast. I decided I would make moonshine. It seemed like a good idea since it was a chemical process. Of course I never did make any whisky, and I told Mrs. Warren a flat-out lie. I wrote-up the project as though I had constructed a whisky still in my backyard and made moonshine. I needed a sample of my product to take to school on project day. Mr. Pierce, a close neighbor, told me I could buy some from Plentis Dupree. I did just that, and Mrs. Warren seemed satisfied! I believe I made at least a "B" on the project. What I had not counted on was Mrs.Warren loading all of her science students on a school bus to travel around the county to view those projects that could not be brought into school. I was a nervous wreck when the bus pulled into Poulan to see Bobby McGirt's fishpond he had made it for his Biology project. I was so afraid she was going to ask to go by my house next to see the moonshine still I had lied about making. I was even more frightened that she and the students would see where I lived. Someone above must have been looking out for me that day since she announced that we had no more time and we had to get back to school. I was very relieved. In retrospect, I wonder whether being out of time was the real reason for Mrs. Warren not taking the class by my house that day. Perhaps, she was aware of my circumstance. If that were the case, I appreciate her for that very much.

One of my earliest encounters concerning the inequitable treatment of Negroes was when I was in the sixth or seventh grade. I was helping our teacher clean out a storage room at Poulan School. We were packing up old school books. Most of the books were ragged without good covers and appeared to be hardly usable. I asked, "What are they going to do with these books"? She said, "We are going to give them to the Negroes". I remembered there was a Negro school across the creek, and I felt a little pang of quilt, even at my age, knowing the old books were not good enough for us but would be alright for the Negroes.

Another incident that aroused my thinking in terms of

equitable treatment of Blacks was when I was working in a grocery store in Poulan. One afternoon, after arriving at work, I was told to clean the meat cooler. There was a refrigerated storage area underneath the lighted display case. I noticed that some of the pork neck bones and spareribs smelled a little peculiar and were a little slick. When I told the owner, "This meat doesn't seem to be good". He said, "Take it outside and wash it off. We will sell it to the Negroes". That incident bothered me immensely and I never could forget it.

I can't recall experiencing any real tensions or conflicts between Blacks and Whites in Poulan before I left for college in 1956. There was an incident that happened to my father once in Sylvester. Daddy came home one Saturday night from Sylvester , and as expected, somewhat drunk. What was unusual was a very noticeable wound on his chin. He told us that he and some friends were walking around the main block of town and he and a young Negro male got into a fight. The fight took place on the sidewalk in front of Miller's Department Store, or close to it. He said some, "Negro Bucks wouldn't step aside and let him pass". When questioned about the cut on his chin he said that the man bit him and he was a "Blue Gum" Negro. Daddy carried that prominent scar on his chin the rest of his life.

It would be several years before integration was established in Georgia when I left for Georgia Teacher's College in 1956. I was enrolled in a freshman English class taught by Mr. Keefer. I believe it was his first year teaching, and he had attended one of the northern universities. Mr. Keefer was a terrific and challenging teacher, and I never regretted being in his class a single minute. He marked us down on incorrect grammar usage but praised us for our thought, content, and originality. He required us to write and to think.

One morning the entire campus was abuzz about a mock hanging of a professor from an oak tree near the entrance to the Administration Building. English courses, among others, were taught in the building. The effigy that was hanged was none other than that of Mr. Keefer. Apparently, he had offended some of his students by espousing anti-segregationist sentiments. I believe it was some of the older males he offended--those returning from the Korean War. His days at Georgia Teachers College were numbered and his contract was not renewed.

I attended his going away party at the end of the term given by some of his students. Mr. Keffer wore his usual bowtie to the party, along with his crew-cut hair, his horn-rimmed glasses and perennial smile. If the loss of his job worried him, he didn't show it. It was then I remembered again, Mrs. Willie Belle Watson's words in the fourth grade as well as the incidents of old schoolbooks and tainted meat at the store. I also remembered one of the songs we sang in chapel at Poulan School. There are several versions of the song I found on the internet. The one below which contains some additional verses is the one that I remember.

### Uncle Ned
There was an old Darkie and his name was Uncle Ned,
And he lived long ago, long ago,
He had no wool on the top of his head
In the place where the wool ought to grow,
(Then lay down your shovel and your hoe-hoe-hoe
Hang up your fiddle and your bow,
For there's no more work for poor old Ned,
He's gone where the good darkies go.)
His fingers were long as the cane in the brake
And he had no eyes for to see,
He had no teeth for to eat a hoecake
So he had to let the hoecake be.
(Then lay down your shovel and your hoe-hoe-hoe
Hang up your fiddle and your bow,
For there is no more work for poor old Ned
He's gone where the good darkies go.)

CHAPTER 9

# Going to the Movies

## Tent Shows

There was no movie theater in Poulan, but tent shows would frequently come to town.  It was an exciting moment when we learned one was being set-up on the large vacant lot between Mr. Alton Gray's grocery store and the old bank on the corner.  The show usually stayed for a week or maybe longer if folks kept coming.  The movies were old black and white westerns from the thirties or maybe earlier.  The sound quality was just a step above that of the silent era. The familiar actors were Hop Along Cassidy, Tom Mix, Sunset Carson, Gene Autry, Lash La Rue, The Durango Kid, Red Ryder, and we mustn't forget The Lone Ranger, Roy Rogers, and several others.

Wood benches were arranged on the left and right of a central aisle.  The film was projected down the top center of the tent, and if tall patrons got up and walked down the aisle, they cast a shadow on the screen.  I remember that African Americans came but have forgotten where they were allowed to sit. They were allowed to sit only in the balcony at the Palace Theater in Sylvester. I believe they were seated in the back of one section of the tent.  Besides proceeds from the small admission, the owners sold popcorn and little boxes of individually wrapped taffy that might come with a prize.  Sometimes, the popcorn was dispensed in long brightly colored transparent paper cone- shaped bags.  I am certain there was no difference, but the popcorn seemed to taste better from those bags. At least it was a good marketing strategy.

If it were winter, the owners had some sort of heater. I remember sometimes a large drum or barrel was outside with a small fire. During summer there was a greater need for air. Very often in hot weather no tent was put up and no admission was charged. Attendance was better when everyone could get in free. These types of shows usually projected the oldest and worst pictures. In addition to popcorn, snow cones and boxed candy, they sold tonic or medicine during a very long intermission. I remember on one occasion a man was hawking a product that would restore and keep hair in a beautiful condition. He extolled the virtues of his product and offered his own head of hair as proof. He said folks washed their hair too often and that wasn't good for hair. He said it had been years since he had washed his own thick black oily mane. A miraculous and versatile tonic was another product sold and was sworn to be a cure-all from arthritis to tired blood. This was not unlike Hadacol that was marketed about that same time. I remember when Mama bought some once and swore it made her feel much better. We later learned it consisted of a large percentage of alcohol (12%). In some states it was allowed to be sold only in liquor stores. Mama still takes pride in saying, "I have never touched a drop of liquor in my life".

### Riding the Train

If we wanted to go to a real Picture Show, we would have to go to Sylvester. The Palace Theater was there and managed by Mr. Luke. It was on the same block with the pool room, bus station and the Woolard Hotel. Mary Nell and I, along with many others from Poulan, hardly missed a Saturday at the Show. There was always a big crowd waiting at the Poulan depot for the noon train to take us to Sylvester. Mr. Potter was the station master and sold us the tickets. I believe he also sent and received messages by telegraph and looked after the freight.

The train engineer started blowing the whistle about when he reached the overhead bridge towards the east to let us know the train was coming. We were already lined-up with ticket in hand and ready to board before the train came to a complete stop. We didn't always calculate correctly just where the boarding door would be in relation to our position in line. Sometimes we were standing in the wrong spot and got a puff of steam as well as some cinders in our eyes. The conductor put out the little stool and helped us aboard. In retrospect, I seriously doubt that he was very glad to see us.

It was always a thrill and new adventure to board the train whether it was going to the Show in Sylvester or on a longer trip with Mama to Macon to see our Great Grandparents Papa and Ma Maude English. During the war years, the train cars were mostly filled with soldiers. If there wasn't a seat available, the soldiers got up and gave Mama a seat when we were on a Macon trip. It made the war a lot more personal for us.

The distance from Poulan to Sylvester was hardly three miles. We were almost there before the train could pick up any speed. We did the things that unsupervised children might be expected to do. We hardly got ourselves seated before we were up again. Our main activity was running to the water fountain at one end of the car. We pulled the little flat paper cups from the dispenser and pushed them open by squeezing the edges. I feel certain that our frequent use of cups and water might have been one of the reasons the trains stopped passing through Poulan. We never took the opportunity to buy fruit, gum, or candy from the man who came around with his box strapped over his neck.

The depot in Sylvester was on the opposite side of the railroad track from the movie. We had to wait for the train to unload the mail and freight and pull out before walking across the tracks and up to the Palace Theater. Mary Nell and I were given fifty-one cents each. I do not know why the extra penny was needed. It was more than enough to get us into the movie and buy a bag of pop-corn and have money left for after the movie. The Saturday movie was always a western and a step above the tent show quality. World War II news was shown along with a cartoon. The best part of the show was the continued serial that kept us coming back. I enjoyed the Tarzan episodes best including quicksand and other danger-ous pitfalls. I can still feel the rope burns in the palm of my hands when I pretended to be Tarzan once and jumped from our tree house to catch a rope tied to a limb. The rope was slick and I im-mediately slid to the ground with aching hands. It was a far worse experience than the time I jumped off the roof of our house with a towel pinned around my neck. Unlike Superman, I couldn't fly, but at least I didn't get any broken bones.

After the movie, we had enough money to go across the street to Deriso Drugs and get a "Crook" and a free glass of wa-ter. A "Crook" was a scoop of vanilla icecream with a squirt of chocolate syrup. It's the same as a chocolate sundae. Sometimes we bought the same at Moore's Drugs or went around to Mullis's Drug Store. We often bought a cherry coke rather than a Crook. We sat at the little marble tables with metal legs as we enjoyed our purchase. The apothecary smell in these places blended with a soda fountain taste isn't an experience that is quickly forgotten.

We still had a good bit of time left before we had to meet the afternoon train to take us back to Poulan. We took this oppor-tunity to go to the dime store and spend the ten cents we had left. We often bought mama a piece of glassware as a butter dish. Some-times we bought a figurine for her to put in her"What Not" cabinet. She had someone convert an old large  battery operated radio on legs into a piece of furniture to display novelties.  I recall several little dogs and such things that used to be in there.

After leaving the dime store, we had time to do what most others did when they came to town on Saturday afternoon. We walked around and around the main business block. Sometimes we reversed our direction and walked around the opposite way. I don't know why we did that. We would meet or pass the same folks several times in a short while. We became familiar with items displayed in the store windows of Miller's Department Store, The Famous Store, Haley's Jewelers and many others. We might have seen who was getting a haircut or shave as we passed McCord's, Willy Floyd,s or the other Barber Shop where John Edward Houston's daddy worked. We passed The Blue Goose and Pop Gullys beer joints. We passed Mr. Gordon Davis's Grocery as well as the larger Harvey's Grocery. We saw lots of cars with folks inside parked in front of the stores. They, too, were also doing what once was a favorite activity on Saturday in Sylvester. They were people watching. When the afternoon train pulled into Poulan, we were on it along with the mail. It was only a short walk to our house since we then lived only a block from the depot in a nice little house across from the water tank. It was another good Saturday spent at the picture show. We had seen previews of the coming attractions, and we hoped Mama would let us go back to the show at least one night during the week. We wouldn't be going on the train but on the back of "Mr. Jim's" truck. She usually let us after wearing her down with our begging.

### Riding with Mr. Jim

Mr. Jim Smith and his wife Ida Pearl lived four houses down from us when we lived in town. They had two children. The oldest was Vera, but everyone called her"Bubba" and she had become blind at the age of sixteen. We were amazed as children that she would know who we were when we spoke to her. She walked by our house often going to town and was usually holding on to some friend who went with her. She was very popular with everyone in Poulan. Billy was her brother and maybe a year or two older than my sister Mary Nell. He was a nice looking boy with a good personality. I never knew what Mr. Jim Smith did for a living other than buy and sell scrap iron and metal during and after the War. Ida Pearl once worked in the cotton mill. I believe she may have started working there when she was a very young girl.  Both Mr. Jim and Ida Pearl were well thought of and were an integral part of the Poulan Community.

Mr. Jim had a booming voice and a good size waist to match. He preferred suspenders rather than a belt and liked to wear a hat.  He wasn't shy and didn't mind telling you what he thought. His truck was in between the size of a pick-up and a two ton farm truck.  It might have been the side bodies that made it look different.  It was an old truck, but he knew how to keep it going. It would be difficult to picture Mr. Jim without his association with the truck.  There was a great need for scrap iron and metal during World War II and even afterwards.  I don't think he got rich from his endeavor, but Mr. Jim made a patriotic effort with buying and selling scrap metal.  As children, we also showed our patriotism by purchasing stamps and placed them in little stamp books.  Unfortunately, we didn't help much since we were too anxious to cash them in at the Post Office.  We never filled up a book.  The post mistress must have been exasperated with our impatience.  We had good intentions, but it was the same as putting money in a savings account one week and taking it out the next.

Mr. Jim liked to go to the Show as much as any of us kids. At least I believe he did.  As soon as we found out he was going to drive his truck to the show that night, we started begging Mama right away to let us go.  If she said she had no money, we reminded Daddy of his "V-Nickel" collection and "Indian Head Pennies". He kept them along with some other coins in a special little black change purse that snapped open and shut.  He hated to part with them, but he sometimes did.  All of those who wanted to go to the show had to be at Mr. Jims house at an appointed time.  Occasionally, he would pick folks up and let them off at other points, but he didn't like to make too many stops.  The crowd varied, but there must have been at least over a dozen folks on back each time he pulled out going to the show.  The distance was short from Poulan to Sylvester and Mr. Jim kept his speed at a cautious level considering the cargo he was carrying. There was lots of excitement on the ride, especially on the return trip when it was darker, but I hesitate to go into any detail.

Being the good business man that Mr. Jim was, he made a deal with the theater manager. He was allowed free admission to the movie due to bringing in so many paying customers. His family members might also have gotten free admission, but I am unsure. The nineteen forties was a golden age for movies with real movie stars. I remember Mary Nell saying one night as we lay in bed, "Wouldn't it be wonderful if we could lay here and watch a movie on the wall when we turned off the lights". Such a wonder did come to pass with the miracle of television. Movie stars were our heroes and a big part of our life. We argued who was the prettiest and which could sing and dance the best. Mary Nell wrote off to Hollywood for autographs of movie stars. She had a good collection. I remember Cornell Wilde, Betty Hutton, Ester Williams, Dale Evans, June Allison, Van Johnson, Jane Russell, Veronica Lake and many others. On my first day in the first grade the teacher asked us to go in front of the room and tell what we wanted to be when we grew-up. I had no trouble doing that and said, "I want to be a movie star". When I told this to my wife later in life, she laughed and said, "But you couldn't have acted in Westerns". "Why"? I asked. "Because you don't have a chin and they would have had a hard time hanging you since the rope would slip off. They would have had to put the rope under your arms if they wanted to hang you," she laughed.

Mr. Jim, Ida Pearl, Bubba, and Billy moved from Poulan to Sylvester by the early nineteen fifties. By that time, my family had already moved into a little mill house that was further away from them down the street. We hated to see them leave. Not only were we losing a ride to the movie but a prominent family as well. The end of an era had come and most of us were growing up by then. We never gave up our love for the Picture Show and we found new ways of getting there.

CHAPTER 10

# Mama's First Refrigerator

On a recent visit to daughter Amanda's large new home in Smyrna, Georgia, I noticed there was very little ice in the ice machine bin. "Is your ice machine already torn up?" I asked. She explained that due to the economic down-turn, they were cutting costs, and she had turned the ice machine on just before I arrived. "It costs fifty cents to a dollar per day for the ice and since we hardly use ice we have begun turning it off. I knew that you would need ice for your scotch and I just turned it on," she said.

This caused my mind to wander back to a time when ice was indeed a major luxury item and when mama made up her mind to buy our first refrigerator. Up until around 1950, we had an icebox and the iceman would deliver a block of ice to fit in the top. Granny and Papa West, my paternal grandparents, did not even have an icebox. I suspect that if they ever owned one it was lost in one of the two house fires that burned them out before I was born in 1938. They had ice only on special occasions. They wrapped the ice in a wool blanket and kept it in a #2 washtub on the back porch. It lasted for a while and the wet blanket was hung on the line to dry.

The only job I ever knew that Mr. Henry Hardage had in Poulan was selling ice. He was the 'ice man' and sometimes his younger son, Charles, would help him. He made rounds on a regular basis. He used large ice tongs to bring a block of ice from his truck into the icebox in our kitchen. I can't remember the size of the block of ice but presume it was a fifty- pound size.

If we needed ice at anytime that did not fit Mr. Henry's delivery schedule, we would have to walk to town to his little icehouse. We walked since we had no car. The icehouse was only a small structure. Ice was stored in it but not made there. The ice was made in a large plant in Sylvester. We had to 'tote' the ice home by hand. Rather than ice tongs, we used some coarse jute string tied around the block to help get it home. We understood that we needed to be quick getting it home before it melted. This presented a problem since ice was in greatest demand on a hot day when water is more quickly changed from the solid to the liquid state. Another problem with children carrying ice is it could get pretty heavy. If we sat it down to rest, it always got dirt on it, and we would have to wash it off when we got home. I can still remember the marks made on the palms of my hands where the jute string cut into them due to carrying the ice too long before resting.

An ice pick was indispensable in every home with an icebox. We learned to pick ice at an early age. Often times, we used the handle of the pick to crack a large piece into smaller ones once we had chipped off a chunk. Ice picks were good to use to punch holes in things such as 'R.C. Cola' bottle tops so the bottle could be used to 'sprinkle-down' clothes before ironing. They could also function as rather notorious weapons. We frequently heard about folks being stabbed with them—right through the heart sometimes or maybe their eyes put out. We learned early to respect the ice pick and use it with caution.

I am certain that most folks who lived on the highway above us who were in better financial circumstances owned refrigerators long before 1950. Maybe even some of the mill families that lived on our street might also have had such a convenience in their kitchen. I was unaware of any if they did. I well remember that "Ma Maude" English, my great grandmother and mama's grandmother in Macon, did have one. It was rather small with a very large motor on the top. I can still remember the smell of her small kitchen with the old gas stove on which she prepared many tasty meals. She also had an indoor bathroom with a commode. The tank was above the toilet and we flushed by pulling a cord. As I recall, the handle was missing and had been replaced with an empty thread spool.

One Saturday, Mama went into the Empire Mercantile Store in Sylvester, a good three miles from Poulan, to look into the possibility of buying our first refrigerator. I am not sure how we got to Sylvester. I suspect we rode with some more affluent neighbors who owned a car. The train and Trailways bus was available, but I am pretty sure we rode with somebody. It could have been Oveda and Frank Touchton our next- door neighbors. They always had a car and maybe this was at the time they had a new Studebaker—the one where the front and back looked the same. Oveda would often drive us to the 'picture show'in Sylvester provided mama would pay their way into the movie. I appreciated going but I was reluctant to sit with them. Their daughter was very fat and I didn't want folks to think I belonged to them. I usually 'held back' and sat by myself under some made up pretense.

Lots of appliances were lined-up on display when we arrived at the Empire Mercantile Co. in Sylvester. Mama's main concern was how she would be able to pay for the refrigerator. She hoped she could put a little down and pay for it on a weekly installment plan. After looking at all the refrigerators on display the salesman acquainted her with a very strategic and clever method of payment. The refrigerators came with an optional electric box or monitor of sorts. In order for the refrigerator to operate, money would have to be put into the meter on a daily or weekly basis. "How much money?" she asked. "Just 25 cents a day—one quarter—would insure that our food would be kept cold and we could have plenty of ice", the salesman said. This was good news to mama and she bought it immediately. I don't know if she made a down payment or not, but the refrigerator was delivered very soon to our little three-room mill house. Mama made certain that she put seven quarters a week in the meter box when she got paid on Friday. A collector from the Empire came around on a regular basis to get the quarters. He carried the coins in a black bag with a tie string. I can't remember how long the man kept coming by for the quarters, but it was a long time I'm sure before the refrigerator was 'paid-off'.

The collection of the refrigerator money was not too different from how our life insurance was paid. Mama put money in a "Life of Georgia" or some other insurance envelop each week. The envelopes hung on a nail just inside the door facing. The 'insurance man' would come around each week, open the door, and take the premium out of the envelope whether we were at home or not. I believe mama cashed-in one of those little life insurance policies to help me start college in 1956 at Georgia Teachers College, which is now Georgia Southern University in Statesboro.

I also recall several other installment type purchases mama made. One of the latest was the merchandise that could be bought from the "L.B. Price Co". They sold bedspreads, electric fans and a variety of other needful things. The collectors were friendly folks who loved to sit a while on the front porch and gossip for a while. I remember a Mr. Turner was an L.B. Price associate. Mama bought a window fan from him. He quit the L.B. Price Co. and opened the skating rink in Sylvester. I believe Queen Altman took his place. She had also been an insurance agent as well, if memory serves me correctly. Regardless, Queen was a very interesting lady with lots of information. Queen was married to mama's sister-in-law's brother. She was practically in the family and that gave way to encouraging lots of talk to which I listened.

The very earliest installment collector I remember was the

man from the "I.P. Rainwater Furniture Company" out of Tifton, Georgia. That is correct," I. P. Rainwater"! It was written on the truck in big letters. Mama bought a bedroom suite off their truck when it came through Poulan during the forties when the war was going on and the mill was working overtime. The suite consisted of a bed, dresser and a chest of drawers. It went well with the old mirrored chiffarobe with a hatbox that we already owned. The bed looked especially good with the peacock bedspread that daddy's niece, Margie, sent to mama form Dalton, Georgia. She was married to a Calloway whose business made the chenille spreads. He was related to Bo Calloway and the owners of Calloway Mills. Mama was real proud of that suite and was hurt to the core when daddy came home drunk one night from the 'Blue Goose' or 'Pop Gulley's' and put his mark on it. I never knew the circumstance that caused the argument, but I saw mama crying after daddy took his pocket- knife and carved a wedge of wood out of the top left edge of the chest of drawers. That "V" shaped scar remained for the life of its existence with us. That was a cruel thing to have done to mama and her new furniture. Mama got rid of the bedroom suite some years ago, but the memory of the scar on the chest and how it got there never went away. It remained an indelible part of my father's legacy. Such terrible meanness was difficult to comprehend.

*Old Poulan Overhead Bridge, Present Day*

*Overhead Bridge minus the Railroad Underneath, Present Day*

CHAPTER 11

# The Overhead Bridge

The overhead bridge in Poulan has been closed to automobile traffic for many years. Barricades erected on each end keeps out motorized vehicles and discourages all but the most determined hiker to walk over the bridge. The trains quit coming through Poulan many years ago and even the railroad tracks have been removed. This wasn't always the case. The bridge located at the east end of Poulan bore heavy traffic until the fifties when highway #82 was rerouted a little distance towards the north past the cemetery and a cotton field. The bridge still remained in use afterwards by a few in town such as the Russell Houston family whose house and a portion of their land was situated just a little east of the bridge. There were also a few folks who lived on an extension of Pepper Street who might also have found it convenient. Even so, very few cars went over the bridge during the day and hardly any at night. From my earliest childhood days, I had heard about the "headless man" who appeared there at night-especially when the trains passed under the bridge below and when children should be in bed. The main purpose of the bridge was to serve as an overpass for the trains that passed through town several times both day and night. The "dinner train" came through from the east at what we now call lunch time at 12:00 noon each day and the "evening train" arrived from the west at approximately 5:00p.m. These brought in the noon and afternoon mail respectively. Freight trains and an occasional "Streamliner" passed through town at other times. The

Streamliners went so fast that we could hardly make out the images of people seated at the windows or in the dining car. We wondered about the destination of those folks who rode the fast trains. We wondered whether they might be from California or New York, or from some other distant place.

The headless man story as told to me has some truth in it. I had always heard that a man jumped from the top of the bridge just as a train was approaching from the other side. He wanted to make sure his death was a certainty. Just recently, I learned from John Porter, a Poulan native, that my information wasn't entirely accurate. When I asked him about it he said, "Mama told me that the man was standing under the bridge behind a pillar with his walking stick. When the train came under the bridge, he jumped in front of it". The story lost a little drama by hearing the man did not jump from the top of the bridge, but I wouldn't dare question Ms. Bessie Porter's version of this suicide. Someone told daddy that the man's pocket watch was still on the front of the train when it stopped in Albany at the train yard. The man who jumped was said to be "Doc Sutton". There was a well known veterinarian who practiced in Sylvester for many years by the name of Dr. Sutton, and it might have been his father or grandfather. I need to check and make sure which generation of Sutton it was.

The "headless man" never showed up when I was there on a dare from Ronnie Hutchinson or from some other boys. Since the ghostly man did not make an appearance, it was perceived to be the incorrect time when the dare was accepted. Ronnie would do almost anything as proof of his bravery. He once climbed to the top of the water tank behind Mr. Kennon's store one night. He said that he wrapped his legs around the ball at the very top of the tank and leaned back with his head and arms pointing down towards the ground. When I went up, I only got as far as the top of the tank. I didn't have the courage to go any further and do what he told us he did.

One afternoon when I was in early grammar school, I recall

going out of my way with some kids to the bridge as we walked home from school. I had accepted their dare to see if I would be brave enough to climb up on a concrete balustrade that lined the sides of the bridge and walk from one end of the bridge to the other without falling to a certain death. The rail road tracks were beneath the middle of the bridge. If I were to fall, I would have chosen to land on the grassy borders and not on the crossties with large granite chunks between them. I took off my shoes and inched my way across the concrete. I didn't look down once I mounted the fortress wall. I kept my eyes off the tracks as I made certain of every step along the top while trying to calm my rapidly beating heart. The potential danger of this walk was much more than seeing how many "cuts" on a railroad track I could walk before falling off. The walk seemed like forever, but I reached the other end of the bridge successfully.

My daring audience had little knowledge of my previous experience of attempting to walk on things above the ground. Once I was caught up in a tight rope walking fantasy after attending a little circus performance earlier one day at Poulan School. After school, I stopped by Bobby McGirt's house to play. With visions of circus acrobatics, I wanted to show him that I could walk across his mother's clothes line that was strung between two pecan trees. My tight rope experience lasted only a few moments before the heavy gauge wire snapped. The fall brought me back to reality. After regaining my breath, I quickly ran on home before Bobby's mother discovered the broken clothes line.

The highway over the bridge was the same highway that we crossed each day on our way to and from school. There was lots of traffic on highway 82, but not nearly as much as there is today on the new four lane road. In the early forties, we sometimes had to wait a while before crossing the highway. This was especially true during the war when a convoy of military vehicles was coming through town on the way to the coast. I recall one afternoon on the way home from school some of us became involved in a potentially dangerous game. The point of the game was to see who could lay down the longest across the white line in the middle of the highway before getting up and running when cars were coming. It was a form of the "chicken game". I am not sure if there was a winner, but I did it and got up and ran just about the time a car reached the front of McGirt's Service Station across from the little Poulan Library. I ran like Hell as the car horn blasted away. This event occurred prior to the creation of the School Safety Patrol which would never have allowed such fool play to take place. The Safety Patrol was composed of more mature and older male students. They wore white belts across their chests with a prominent badge.

The best use I found for the bridge during my adolescent years was a place of refuge and reflection when my life seemed hopeless and at the very worst. I went there many times both day and night to find solace and comfort. It was especially peaceful to be alone up on the bridge at night with a full moon out and with many stars aglow. It was a place for pondering and solitude . It was one of my sanctuaries. One could see vast distances from the lofty perch of the bridge. The only souls around were those in the city cemetery only a few steps away. This would have been a perfect time for the " headless man" to have made himself known to me had he the desire. A ghost story was the least of my worries at those points of my life. I wondered about myself and how I fit into the scheme of things. It was difficult to think positively when I found myself in such a seemingly hopeless and negative environment. I needed the protection and security that the bridge offered. As I leaned on the concrete rails they might have felt warm or cool depending upon the season and time of day but they always felt solid. I needed that feeling. I usually came away from the bridge with a little better outlook and reassurance. The overhead bridge was like "Possum Poke" which was another important personal refuge in times of turmoil. They both were "getting my head in gear" places and allowed me to "keep on keeping on".

On numerous occasions, I found the bridge to be a quiet

and romantic destination when I had the opportunity of female companionship. The earliest remembrance was of a girl who was visiting a family that was big in the Baptist Church. She was thin with short black hair and wore high heels. She played the piano and sang extremely good solos in church on Sunday evenings. She and I made several visits to the bridge after the night service . She seemed to like some elementary poetry of mine . She was a deeply religious girl with a serious outlook on life. She gave me a little book authored by Danforth with the title of "I Dare You". It was about leading the four square life which pertained to our social, spiritual, physical, and intellectual wellbeing and development. I remember that my sister read it and became bold enough to finish high school through correspondence and go on to several other pursuits. It would be remiss not to mention that this female summer visitor in Poulan was in the possession of another talent. She was a very good and experienced kisser. As our visits to the bridge became more frequent, our talk of poetry and philosophy became so much less significant than our kissing.

There were a few other girls that accompanied me to the bridge, but the last one was the girl I married in 1960. I took her there at night to share my old place of comfort and silence. I told her of the importance of the bridge to me during earlier years and some of the dreams I had. I told her the bridge had been so important that I wanted my ashes scattered from there at night. I have a feeling that she wasn't too impressed with my drama and theatrics, but she endured it all. I also carried her to "Possum Poke," but it wasn't as romantic during the day light hours.

We often talked of having a "Bridge Party"--not one of card playing, but a real party with all the expected trimmings. We will have been married fifty-one years this April of 2011, and I rather suspect that party might not take place. The scattering of ashes from the bridge seemed like good drama at the time but most likely won't occur--not because it has become useless and abandoned, but because I am searching for a more appropriate and better place as I grow older.

*Charles Luther West Grave Stone, Red Oak Graveyard*

CHAPTER 12

# They Killed Luther

It was early on a cold January morning in 1951 when Mama came into the room where Troy and I were snuggled in bed, "Get up, get up", she said franticly. I was only half awake as she began throwing my covers back. "Luther is dead!" "He was shot and killed last night!" "I want you to go up to the McCrarys and call Lucy Maude and let them know"!

Luther was my uncle and my daddy's brother. It reads on his grave that he was born in 1903, however, I am fairly certain he was born in 1908 according to several census records. Daddy was born in 1911 which made him three years younger. Luther and Daddy married sisters Lucy Maud and Janie (Polly) Fambro. Luther and Lucy had three children who were the same ages as Mama's and Daddy's three children making us double first cousins. Such cousins are more genetically linked than normal first cousins. Our families were not only genetically close but also close in a physical and emotional way. This was especially true in the early years. Both families began their lives on neighboring farms as share croppers north of Doles, Georgia. There were three children in each family with the oldest of each born in 1935 followed by the middle two born in 1938 and the last two in 1940. When Mama's and Lucy's parents died, their youngest sibling, Mary Ethel, moved in with Luther and Lucy while their youngest two brothers,

Clarence and Ray, moved in with Mama and Daddy. Both families gave up share cropping and moved to work in the Poulan Cotton Mill at about the same time in the early 'forties'. Towards the late 'forties, Aunt Lucy Maud divorced Luther and packed up her sister and three children and moved to Manchester, Georgia to work in the Calloway Cotton Mill. Her brother, Uncle Clarence Fambro, had already moved up there with a job at the mill and helped her get started with a new life.

I got quickly dressed and started up the road to the Mc-Crary house to use their phone. Very few homes had telephones in Poulan even though it was 1951. I don't recall any of the mill houses having them at the time. Mr. McCrary lived a couple of blocks up the street in town. His house was quite nice with a lovely yard. I believe he had once owned all of the houses on his side of the block. I know Mama bought the first house she owned from him which was three doors up from his and closer to town. It was much larger and nicer than what we had to move into after Daddy kept "hounding" her to sell it. Mama still owed Mr. McCrary and It had been my task to deliver several hundred dollars down to him when she sold our house to Mr. Sego.

Whereas I had walked by the McCrary house on a daily basis for years, I had never been beyond the front porch. Mr. Goston McCrary and his wife would just about always be sitting on their front porch as I passed and we would nod and say hello. They were much older with white hair and had children as old as my parents. I was a little hesitant when I knocked on their front door so early that morning. Mrs. McCrary came to the door and invited me in after learning of my mission. I am not sure if her husband heard me because he didn't come into the room. Perhaps he had not yet put in his hearing aid that he always wore. Mrs. McCrary lead me into the dining room where the telephone was attached to the wall. I believe Sherriff Hudson's wife was the operator in Sylvester we had to go through in order to make the call.

Aunt Lucy had been fortunate in finding a mill house in Manchester to move into with her three children and young sister. Not only did the larger mill houses have bathrooms but she was also able to get a telephone. The Callaway Mills complex was much more expansive than the Poulan Cotton Mill. There was a wonderful recreational facility, "The Y", with a swimming pool close by their house. They lived within walking distance to the thriving town center which had its own movie theater. My siblings and I spent several happy summers visiting in Manchester, Georgia. I don't recall much about my conversation with Lucy Maude other than Luther had been shot and killed the night before. "All Mama said was he had been killed by some of that gang near Pepper Street", I told her. I do remember that Mrs. McCrary didn't leave the room and kept a close ear to the conversation. I presume getting some news in this fashion was one of the perks for the few folks with the luxury of a telephone.

The next couple of days were anxious times. Mama and daddy had to take charge of making funeral arrangements. Daddy was visibly shaken over the incident and tried to do his best. This was unusual for him since he seemed to care little for our family needs in the way a husband and a father should. As I grew older, he spent more time in the Blue Goose beer joint in Sylvester than at home. He was certain that Luther had been murdered in cold blood and the killers should be brought to justice. He went more than once to the crime scene to seek explanation and evidence. All he could gather from a crying female resident is Luther was drunk and tried to break into the house and get to her for sex. They had to kill him to make him stop. The scene was located down a sandy dirt road off the east end of Pepper Street. It was nothing more than a rundown house with a nearby tar paper shack or two in which folks might sometime live. One of the shacks was across the road. According to memory, there was one or two primary families associated with the property, but the census varied from time to time as to exact number and names of occupants and their associates.

Daddy discovered they had swept the front yard before daylight. He was sure this was done in order to hide evidence that the body had been dragged through it from the actual shooting site. I also remember him bringing in a piece of torn beaver board with shot gun holes in it taken from another place on the property. He intended to use it as proof that a murder had occurred. Daddy didn't trust the lawyers in Sylvester to take his case. He thought that the sheriff and the law was somehow tied in with bootlegging and the gang. He went to Tifton, Georgia to try to find a lawyer but nothing ever became of it. Daddy had no money, no transportation, and very little education for such a pursuit. The last I remember hearing of any activity was when Daddy brought Jack Sumner into our house to show him the old piece of shot-up board he had. Jack Sumner was campaigning for Worth County Sheriff against Mr. Hudson at the time and indicated he would take a look into the situation if elected. He wasn't elected and that pretty much concluded Daddy's efforts.

I could be mistaken, but it was fairly common knowledge that the men folks, along with their friends and associates were involved with "moon-shinning", poker playing , and maybe other nefarious activities. I do recall observing a county deputy sheriff make contact one night with one of these characters. Some claim there might have been pay-offs between the "shiners" and the law. Poker playing was illegal and always took place down in the woods and under the cover of darkness. As children, we often saw signs that a poker game had been played when we walked the bank under the bridge over the creek. There were scattered bottles, some cards, and half burned wood around the site. I have good knowledge in my later years that these gatherings might parallel some of the activities described in the novel, "Deliverance", by James Dickey. However, unlike the novel, the victim in this case was a willing participant.

A few years prior to Luther's death, another man was found dead on the railroad track near Poulan. He was from an important family in town and had a wife and children. Whereas it was never proved, there was a strong belief that the man had been killed by some of the same crowd connected with Luther's death. It was talked around town that the man was killed in a drunken poker brawl and the killers placed his body on the railroad tracks so it would appear that he died from being run over by the train. It was of interest to learn that one of the supposed participants was found murdered down in Mexico a few years later. He held no kinship to the rest of the group and was an absentee father of one of my childhood acquaintances being raised by his grandparents.

Uncle Luther was a mean man and I tried to avoid him as often as possible. Mama said he hadn't been right after being cut in the head from a sawmill accident before moving to Poulan. I say he was just mean to the core. Luther got even meaner when he was drunk. I witnessed at least one brawl between him and daddy one night. They were rolling all over the front yard "cussin" and swinging fists. Mama also told me later in life why Lucy left him. "He was always trying to "get with" Mary Ethel, she said. "Get with" was Mama's way of saying he was trying to have sex with his young sister-in-law who was living with them. Mama went on to say, "She found him out in the corn field one day with her and she picked up a big stick and threatened him". Mama continued, "After moving to Poulan, he kept on bothering Mary Ethel while she was in high school and Mary Nell said he tried to get her into bed with him". Mary Nell was my sister for Heaven's sake! I also previously heard about Luther taking advantage of an elementary age girl not long before he was killed.

Luther did not like the idea of Lucy leaving him as he tried to adjust to the life of a single man. He continued to work in the cotton mill but had to give up the little mill house since he had no family. He moved in with "HD" who had half a house on Pepper Street. Half a house meant two rooms consisting of a combination living-bedroom plus a kitchen. "HD" had been in World War II. I am uncertain whether he completed his stint in the service.

It wasn't obvious, but he would have fit into the, "Don't Ask-Don't Tell" category had that been in place during his enlistment. He also kept a close relationship with some of the poker playing gang. I do remember he looked after his mother when she was very ill and dying with cancer. He had a sister in town, but she offered little care for their mother. This is the place where Luther was living when his oldest son, Farrell, and I walked down the railroad tracks to see him. Farrell had come from Manchester to visit with us that summer. I don't recall much about the visit other than one frightening incident. Before we left, Luther pulled out a pistol and said to his son, "This is for your Mama". "I don't know when or where, but I'm going to kill her".

Sometime later, Luther and his housemate moved into a little shack across the road up in a pecan orchard. There was a very large mulberry tree to one side of the property that I remember eating from as I delivered papers. I went inside once while Luther was there. Everything was so dark and dismal with minimal furnishings beyond two iron frame beds. Luther had lost the use of one of his eyes for some reason. His eyeball was removed and he had a glass eye instead. While I was trying to leave, Luther reached for his prosthetic eye stored in a glass of water on the mantle--as some do with their false teeth. He dropped the eye on the floor while trying to put it into his socket. He quickly picked up the thing and placed it into his mouth and rolled it around. I don't know if he was trying to clean it or get some spit on it so he could make it fit better. It was a disgusting sight and it was about the last time I remember seeing him before he was laid out in his coffin in our front room.

Mama and Daddy brought Luther home from Banks Funeral Home in Sylvester. It was customary for a wake to be held in the family home during those years. We were his only family in Poulan, so it fell upon us to hold it at our house. There was no room for a casket in our little front room that served as Mama's and Daddy's bed room plus the family sitting area. It was just one of three rooms. They dismantled their bed and put the casket in its place. There was enough room left for some folding chairs the funeral home furnished along with any flowers and the "sympathy sign-in stand". I don't know whether Mama and Daddy slept with Troy and me in our room that night. Neither do I remember who "sat-up" with the corpse or if it turned into a two- night affair. I only re-member going to Red Oak Baptist Church near Doles, Georgia for the funeral. He was laid to rest by his parents, Charlie and Amanda West, out in the cemetery so familiar to me as a child when my sister and I visited our grandparents when Papa was caretaker of the church's grave yard. I wish I could recall any good words the preacher might have said about him during the service, but I can't. I have little concern whether Luther was murdered or not. Did he deserve to die when considering his lifestyle and some terrible deeds he had done? Was his killing justified? I can't answer those questions. I can only say that it must be a terrible legacy to leave this world with no one remembering any good or love for this man.

*Big Poke*

*Little Poke*

CHAPTER 13

# Possum Poke

Stories from Poulan would be very incomplete without mention of "Possum Poke in Possum Lane." Possum Poke was the winter home of Governor Chase Salmon Osborn. He was a one term governor of Michigan in 1911-1913. The Governor and a group of men from Michigan came to the area in search of timber. They discovered quail in Poulan and built a lodge they named "Hungers Camp." The Governor bought out the shares of the other owners over a period of time until he was the sole owner. He experienced a rich and fascinating journey between his birth in 1860 in Indiana and his death at Possum Poke in 1949. He was much more than a politician and statesman. A naturalist, world traveler and explorer, newspaper man and publisher, author, philosopher and philanthropist are among the terms used to characterize him.

Possum Poke was actually a compound consisting of several buildings and structures. After the realignment of Highway #82, the entrance into "Possum Lane" is just a few steps from the west bound lanes of the highway. This narrow lane today is lined with a much less dense growth of trees than in earlier days. There is a second, newer entrance opposite the little roadside park. Actually, this is part of a field road that parallels some of the original Possum Lane at its southern terminus. The realignment of Highway #82 cut through the southernmost portion of the property. Stellanova had the State Highway Department construct a roadside park on that portion opposite the highway. A granite memorial to the Governor is placed there along with several picnic tables. The driveway and parking areas are lined with rocks. Recently, Richard Sumner told me that his father, Jack Sumner, had donated these rocks from their family farm in Worth County. Even more of Possum Poke was consumed when the highway was expanded into four lanes. The second section was added closer to "Little Poke". Stellanova wrote a note to me saying that she had fought the highway for taking more of Possum Poke, "But they decided the "car graveyard" on the opposite side was of more importance to save than that of her beloved residence," she said.

From its original entrance, Possum lane makes a right turn in front of the larger house and narrows a bit more before reaching the smaller one. The Governor had the habit of re-naming things, places, and people. He named the larger two story house "Big Poke" and the smaller cottage, some distance to the left, "Little Poke." The persimmon tree in Possum Lane was the inspiration for "Possum", and "poke" means a sack. Before his health failed, the Governor and Stellanova stayed in Big Poke. Afterwards, they resided in Little Poke. Big Poke had upstairs guest rooms which were frequently used by "important" and "not so important" persons, particularly during hunting seasons when he was younger. Cooking and dining also took place in Big Poke. The kitchen, along with the cook's living quarters, was attached to the rear of the main house by an enclosed breezeway. The well for drawing water was also located there along with pie safes and storage cabinets. The furniture was basic to the needs of residents and guests. There was a long wood table surrounded by rather plain chairs in the dining room. The wood walls, like all others in the house, were unpainted. However, they held several varied pieces of memorabilia from places far and wide. I recall a very large carved wood spoon and fork displayed on the dining room wall. The dining room was a front room on the right side of the house and could also be entered from a right front porch door. The left front porch door led into a large room equivalent in size to the dining room. This is where I remember visiting with Stellanova after the Governor's death. It no doubt was much like the Governor left it. She slept there and did a tremendous amount of correspondence and writing on a very old typewriter kept on a small desk. I recall seeing his old wheelchair upon which Stellanova had attached a flower corsage. It must have been there for quite some time since it resembled flowers that had been dried and pressed in thick books as the Bible. Several photos and newspaper clippings were taped to the wall. The kitchen was equipped with a cast iron wood burning stove. A wood box was in the breezeway that held the fuel that fed the fireplaces in the major rooms, at least, in the early days.

Little Poke was a single story cottage a good distance to the left of Big Poke. The grounds between the two houses were planted with a variety of trees and shrubs-- some native, others imported. I remember Spanish Bayonet everywhere. However, it was not as prolific as the wisteria that grew rampant up and over the canopy of trees. There was a long arbor next to Little Poke made of wire and steel that was also covered in wisteria. It was a thrill walking underneath upon a thick carpet of fallen wisteria blossoms. I have never smelled any sweeter smell than at Possum Poke during wisteria season. A flag pole was positioned at the approximate center between the two houses. Raising and lowering of the flag was performed daily when the Governor and Stellanova were in residence. She continued the practice after his death. It was a ceremonial event conducted with high reverence and patriotic fervor. Presently, there are two granite head stone type markers near the flag pole, one commemorating Chase S. Osborn and the other Stellanova. They do not mark grave sites since both are buried on Duck Island in Michigan near Sault Ste Marie.

Little Poke was a cozy structure with a very large library-office room on the front. It was equipped with a prominent stone fireplace and a large desk. It housed numerous books, photos, and memorabilia. This is where they worked and wrote. There was a wood deck on the south side of Little Poke where the Governor enjoyed sunning himself and observing the distant woods in the winter season. Additionally, the house was used as sleeping quarters for them in later years. Most prominent among the other buildings was the "hot house" with its many windows where exotic plants, as orange trees, were kept free from winter's cold. There were also some storage buildings along with the chicken houses. Turkeys roosted in the trees at night but flew down at day break always ready to gobble for those who came down Possum Lane. In the early years, there was a barn with cows. "Bovina" was the nick name given to Ethel Rhymes, who I remember most, as the last cook and helper at Possum Poke. Bovina got her name from an interesting story concerning a calf. There were other persons of interest during Possum Poke's grand days. "Mammy", old "Gobbin", and Bovina are among several characters Stellanova describes in her book, "A Tale of Possum Poke in Possum Lane." Possum Poke was much like a small plantation during the early days. Most food items were either raised on the place or hunted close by. The hunting dogs were of upmost importance to the Governor and Possum Poke. They weren't human, but according to Stellanova, Mammy almost designated "Old Nog" that status when she said, "He thinks he's folks."

I believe I was about ready for the first grade and the Governor already a wheelchair bound old man when I first saw him and heard his name. At the time, we were living in the John Gray house which is on one of the primary north-south streets and near the center of Poulan. Several of us children were playing in the yard when we heard a great deal of commotion. "The Governor is coming, the Governor is coming", we heard someone say. We ran out to the road and sure enough, there was a band of strange looking folks coming toward us. They had gotten off the train at the depot and had already passed Mr. Goodman's Drug Store. They were different from the usual passengers. There was an American Indian, or perhaps two, pushing the Governor in a wheel chair. You could tell they were Indians because of their dress, hair, and color. A strange looking woman, later learned as Stellanova, was walking close behind and dressed in high top tennis shoes, thick stockings and wearing a mariner's hat over her short cropped hair. The Governor had the same type shoes and hat and they both wore thick glasses. The only paved street in Poulan during that time was the highway. It must have been difficult to push the Governor in that old narrow gauge wheel chair all the way out to Possum Poke."Uncle Charlie Merritt" was their usual chauffer when they were in residence. According to his nephew, John Merritt, he drove a large black Cadillac that he had bought from the Governor. John said that his Uncle Charlie was somewhat of a caretaker along with driving the folks at Possum Poke. I don't know why he wasn't there that day to drive them. Perhaps the Governor, being such an avid outdoorsman, wanted the fresh air since the train trip had been long and exhausting coming all the way from Michigan to Poulan.

Later as children, some of us would be brave enough to go out to visit the governor. We heard how rich he was, and we had high expectations that he would give us some money. It was probably my sister, Mary Nell, who hatched the idea. If it wasn't, it sounds like something she would do, so I am crediting her with the deed. When Mary Nell and I arrived at Big Poke, we noticed Stellanova pushing the governor in his wheel chair out in the yard. I remember feeling a little frightened and timid, but with Mary Nell's prodding, I said, "We have come to see how the governor is feeling today." I don't remember how long we visited, but Stellanova was very cordial as she led the conversation between all parties. I distinctly remember that upon leaving Possum Poke, we were each given a nickel along with a small scrawny orange plucked from a greenhouse tree. This was little reward for a long walk out to the place. A nickel would buy a nice ice cream cone, but it wasn't quite enough for the cost of a ticket to get into the show.

When I was a little older in the mid forties, I went with daddy out to the place. He was hired to shave the Governor on a periodic basis. I believe Daddy was paid fifty cents per visit. I forget how long Daddy's grooming job lasted, but I do remember him coming home and remarking how the old man would cuss when he nicked him a time or two. Once daddy brought home a very large green book that Stellanova and the Governor had given him. It was the thickest and heaviest book I had ever seen and would have been ideal for flower pressing. Even though Daddy, with his fourth grade education, read "Readers Digest", "The Grit" paper, and several other magazines, I never saw him read in that big book. It was so heavy that Mama might have even used it to help press her souse meat or hog head cheese she made each year around Christmas. The book was compiled and edited by Stella (Stellanova) Brunt Osborn in 1940 with 605 pages. The title was almost as long as the book was thick, "An accolade for Chase S. Osborn. Home, State, and National Tributes on the Occasion of Chase S. Osborn Day, October 4, 1939." This was a compilation of testimonials in the Governor's honor.

It is true that Governor Osborn had made a great deal of money during his life time. It is also true that he gave most of it away. It would be difficult to trace and document the beneficiaries of his many philanthropic activities. The exploration and production of iron ore was one of his chief money making ventures. He traveled at home and abroad in search of the ore. One of the books he authored, "The Iron Hunter", is autobiographical and describes his pursuit and interest in that resource. He had a great interest in education and gave generously to several universities in Michigan. There are monuments in his name as well as a residence hall. The governor and Stellanova both loved and wrote poetry. I read recently that he sponsored the poet, Robert Frost, as a "Poet in Residence" at the University of Michigan. Worth County was a benefactor of the governor's benevolence. Camp Osborn, a Boy Scout camp in the north-west corner of Worth County, is named for the man who gave several hundred forested acres to the area Boy Scouts in the 1940's. When some area men approached him for donating a few acres, the Governor said, "Why don't you ask for the whole thing?" Another no less important contribution, but perhaps less known, was his financial underwriting of the publication of "History of

Worth County, Georgia" by Lillie Martin Grubbs and the local DAR.

Scouting and Camp Osborn brings to mind my days as a Boy Scout in Poulan. We were a struggling group from the very beginning. Our little Scout troop in Poulan would have a sudden burst of interest and activity followed by a period of "do nothing". I am uncertain as to who began our first efforts. Dan Smith is the first troop leader that comes to mind. Dan was a veteran of World War II. He married Becky from Doerun and she shared her new husband generously with the troop. We were in and out of their house quite often. He was the first to carry us on an overnight camping trip. Dan was a good gardener and held an avid interest in flying motorized model air planes. I remember eating a spam sandwich made with lettuce and green onions from his garden. I still like spam when it is chilled and sliced real thin. My family thinks I am crazy for eating such. Maybe most of its goodness is nostalgic. I also enjoy a can of small sardines with hot sauce. I ate lots of Vienna sausage until I read on the label that they contained beef lips. If I blot that out, I still might eat one or two.

Buck Hutchinson was among the last troop leaders during my time. He, too, was a World War II Veteran and the brother-in-law to Dan Smith. Buck was a plumber by trade. One of our troop's money making projects was digging holes for septic tanks on two jobs where Buck was doing the plumbing on houses that Lacy Welch was building. Several of us worked very hard digging those holes in clay. One was at the house in which Mama lives today across from the Poulan Baptist Church. The other is the house next door to the right of hers. After we finished our project, Buck promised to take us on an all expense paid overnight trip to Jacksonville Beach, Florida. Not too long afterwards and true to his word, Buck took us to the beach. He found rooms in a house near the beach and gave us money for supper. We had a real adventure and for most the beach was a new experience. Buck was a great guy but I disliked his teasing. I pretended it didn't bother me, but it always did.

During one of our Scout meetings held at the little one-room Poulan Court House, it was decided our troop needed some financial help. A plan was made where I would visit Stellanova Osborn at Possum Poke to see if she had any suggestions for the troop's fund raising. We were hoping that she would just give us some money. After all, the Governor had already given all that land for the Boy Scout Camp and surely we felt as though she might give us a sizable donation. I should have remembered my earlier childhood visit concerning the nickel and the orange. Stellanova was of the opinion that the best way to raise funds was to work for them. Such a person and philosophy, if placed as head of certain governmental programs, would be of tremendous benefit in today's world. She went to a large box and pulled out several books. These were of her recently published works of poetry. One was, "Jasmine Springs" and the other, "Beside the Cabin". She said the troop could have the money, or some portion, for each copy sold. I do not remember how much they cost nor whether we sold any of them. I probably returned just about as many as she gave me. I did keep a copy of each of the small paperback books for myself. She had even autographed the "Jasmine Springs" copy. I still have these little books of poems and enjoy reading them from time to time. In spite of my meager fund raising efforts, I was beginning to take a liking to Stellanova. One of her little poems in "Jasmine Springs" comes to mind.

Evolution
Blooded cats may sniff at Kings
Whose crowns are gone.
Any country mouse can sneeze
At a mastodon.

She was a most unusual person. She thought and spoke on a grander level than mine. Understandably, she should have since she was a university graduate who spoke several languages and who had been the Governor's researcher and secretary. She corresponded and met with political figures at home and abroad. Much of what she spoke of was beyond my grasp, but I liked her manner and seemingly genuine interest in so many things beyond the scope of ordinary life in Poulan and Worth County. She spoke to me as if I were as knowledgeable as any noted political figure. She smiled a lot as she talked intensely with both her eyes and voice. I always came away feeling somewhat different, even though it might take a while in attempting to digest the entire visit and conversation that I had with her.

I never got to know the Governor in any personal way before he died in 1949. I was eleven then and had paid only a few short visits to Possum Poke. I believe I saw him last when he was in his wheel chair at the supper table in the dining room of Big Poke. It was much before dark, but the Governor operated on a different time schedule from everyone else. He was a few hours ahead of normal and got up way before dawn. I do not remember the reason for my visit. I do remember that he was eating a plate of rice and tomatoes, almost like tomato and rice soup. Bovina was there along with Stellanova.

I had a greater opportunity after the Governor's death to get to know Stellanova. When I think of Possum Poke, I think of Stellanova and I see the face of a most unusual person. I also regret that I did not take more initiative in forming a closer relationship with her. The Governor met Canadian, Stella Brunt, in 1924. He hired her to do research and become his secretary. After a few years, the Governor and his wife, Lillian, adopted her in 1931. Stella was thirty-seven years old at the time. She took the name of Osborn and it was the Governor who quickly named her Stellanova. She was his constant helpmate and companion. She took on the duty of his nurse when he became wheelchair bound. I have read that Stellanova's adoption was annulled after the death of the Governor's wife; however, I do not know the extent of time between his wife's death and the annulment of adoption. I do know that local tongues were wagging when Stellanova married the Governor on his death bed two days before he died at Possum Poke in April of 1949. Some folks considered the marriage of the Governor to his adopted daughter bordered on incestuous behavior. She was fifty-four and he was eighty-nine at the time. The most confounding and troublesome thing about their relationship is a lack of any written word about their love for each other. I have read numerous newspaper articles as well as information from the internet but am yet to read anything suggestive of a romantic relationship.

I have always believed an epic novel or television series could be developed around the lives of the Governor and Stellanova. He was a man born in 1860 to abolitionists parents. His very name, Chase Salmon, comes from an abolitionist. He is a young man who meets and deals with the many challenges of making his way in the world. He is an outdoorsman and a naturalist like Teddy Roosevelt. He is a news reporter and publisher of newspapers. He searches for timber and iron ore. He becomes wealthy and he enters politics. He was on several governmental boards before becoming the Governor of Michigan. He "hob- knobs" with leaders and others he considers worthwhile for a country and cause. He is among the last of our pioneers. (Some of his life not known to me enters here.) There is his wife Lillian, and his children and grandchildren to reckon with in this saga. Who was she? Where was she? What was she doing during all this time, especially after Stellanova came into the picture? In contrast to this masculine giant is our heroine, Stellanova, who must have been smitten with him from the beginning. He was a robust and handsome man before his wheelchair days. He must have been attracted to her intellect in the beginning, although earlier photos of her don't do her any dishonor. She was by his side and his second voice in the latter days. What was she in their beginning and middle days? Was she like Stella in "Streetcar Named Desire"? They traveled far and wide together meeting dignitaries and common folk alike. Just how physically passionate were they--if they were at all?

They had shared passions and visions for many things. There was a love of ideas, writing and poetry. They so loved everything about nature, its rhythms and its relationship with human kind. They disliked war and were passionate in their desire to end tyranny and bring about peace. Whereas a relationship devoid of physical expression is possible, it would seem unrealistic during their twenty-five years together. It is evident through some of her poems and writings that she dearly loved the Governor. She remained close and caring during his old age when he might become grouchy with loss of temper and understanding. She never left his side in bad times and even shortly after his death. At his death in 1949, the Governor's body was placed on a train in Worth County, Georgia and sent back to be buried on Duck Island near Sault Ste. Marie, Michigan. According to the Osborn's attorney in Sylvester, Mr. Joe Houston, Stellanova rode back with him on the same train--not in the passenger car, but all the way sitting in a chair beside his casket in another car. This almost exceeds the limit of devotion in my estimation.

Stellanova continued a very active life after the Governor's death. She wrote and published works of poetry. She devoted the greatest amount of time to "Atlantic Union" that she found, or help find, in 1958. She spent many years working for the Union of Democracies. Her work with this organization required her to live in Washington, DC. She had no salary or expense account and very often visited all the NATO countries in the interest of the organization and its cause. I still have a picture post card she sent me from Iceland. Possum Poke had been her primary residence until about 1982 when she decided, due to health reasons, to make her permanent residence in Sault Ste. Marie, Michigan. She died March 3, 1988 at the age of ninety-three.

In 1965 Stellanova deeded Possum Poke to Abraham Baldwin Agriculture College to care for and help preserve its place in history. I do not know any present details. I have heard that ABAC had rented it to Worth County some years ago. I also know that private individuals have lived there, at least in Little Poke, on some occasions. When I stopped by recently and peered through the windows of Little Poke, I saw that Boy Scout materials were in the large library. Perhaps the local troop is meeting there now. If so, this would be a very fine tribute to the Governor and Stellanova. Whereas a little work has been done to shore-up Little Poke, it seems there is a lack of interest and resources in restoration of the remainder of the place. It appears to be falling down.

It is so sad to see such an important piece of Worth County fall into ruin. It is especially discomforting to me since this was a major place of refuge and solitude during my formative years. It is hard to estimate the number of visits I made to Possum Poke when I was alone, even though I never seemed to be alone at that place. There seemed to be some pervasive force that soothed my greatest anxieties and directed my thoughts toward a better perspective. It was among "my getting my head in gear places". It had a calming effect and was a religious experience of the first order.

*Georgia Tearchers College became Georgia Southern in 1959*

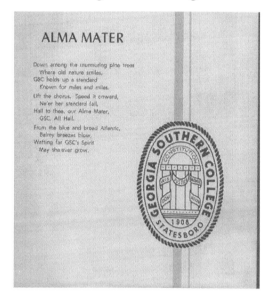

CHAPTER 14

# Starting College and Going to California

I met Wallis DeWitt in the fall of 1956 when I entered Georgia Teachers College in Statesboro as a freshman. The college was re-named Georgia Southern College during the time I was there. It is now known as Georgia Southern University. When I graduated in 1960, the enrollment was less than a thousand. This is considerably below the present enrollment of around twenty times that num-ber. Wallis was a sophomore and had already been there for a year before my arrival. He was quick in dispensing a wealth of informa-tion about the "ins and outs" of college life as well as the "do's and don'ts" of my new venture.

Wallis and I were "almost roommates" since we had rooms next to each other in Sanford Hall that housed freshman and sophomore males. Cone Hall was a newer dorm next door where the junior and senior men lived. My roommate was Bobby Mc-Girt from Poulan. Bobby and Jeanette Branch were the only two students who began school with me in the first grade in Poulan and remained with me through graduation from Sylvester High School in 1956. Bobby and I continued our academic association for almost two more years as roommates before he dropped out of college toward the end of his sophomore year. I never knew exactly why Bobby quit college. He was far more intelligent than I was in areas like mathematics. He must have had better math genes than I did since we both had the same math teachers. I would never have passed College Algebra that first quarter had he not allowed me to copy his homework almost every night. Ms. Viola Perry was the Registrar of the college and also taught us Algebra. Wallis called her "Sugar Bugger". I don't remember why he called her by that name. We did not use a text book, but she gave us five problems each night to solve. They were the hardest problems one could imagine. After hours of frustration, I always called upon Bobby for help. I made a "B" in that class only because fifty percent of the grade came from homework that I copied from Bobby. I still have nightmares about that class. I often dream that I am about to graduate from college, but I have to pass the final algebra exam. The exam is today, but I don't know where it is since I have never been to class. When I awake from this nightmare, I am so proud that I am back in the real world and not taking college algebra.

Wallis told me a funny story that happened when he took Ms. Perry's class the year before. He told me about an old farm boy who was in the class with him. Wallis said Ms. Perry called upon the boy to answer a question and the boy said, "Hell woman, I had just soon be out in the field plowing my mule as sitting in here". Without saying another word, the boy just got up and walked out of the classroom and went back home to the farm.

I was so excited to go to college. I worked in the Poulan Cotton Mill and other places to make money during the summer to buy clothes for college in the fall. Mama cashed-in a small life insurance policy she had on me so that I could get started the first quarter. My brother-in-law had given me an old metal trunk from the WWII era, and I kept it in my room in our little three room house in the mill village. Each week, I would buy some article of clothing and lay it away in the old trunk. I can still smell the newness of those things along with the moth balls as I repeatedly opened the heavy trunk and looked with eager anticipation on the

day I would wear them. I might have rearranged and patted them
down a bit. I suppose it wasn't unlike a "Hope Chest" that girls
used to keep before their marriage. I had several shirts, trousers,
underwear, and socks. I believe I wore "Fruit of the Loom" briefs
back then. My final wardrobe addition was a dress suit. I bought
the suit in Columbus, Georgia on Broad Street from the Schwobilt
factory store. I had passed the store numerous times as I walked
from my sister's house on Front Avenue up town to the movie.
Their motto was "Schwobilt Suits the South". It was a classic dark
gray with subtle stripes. The coat had three buttons and there
was a small ivy league belt below the waist in back of the pants. It
reminded me of the light blue denim "pegs" Bill McCord and I
bought at Goldsmith's in Albany during 1955-56. They too had a
little belt in back and they were pegged at the bottom. That suit
carried me through four years of college.

I supplemented the suit with the white linen jacket I wore
to the Junior-Senior Prom in both the eleventh and twelfth grades.
It might have had some stains left around the lapel from the red
carnation boutonnieres. I also carried along the black and white
shoes that went well with the coat at formal college dances. Then
too, there was the pink and charcoal sport coat that I wore with
my long sleeve pink dress shirt with French cuffs that went very
well with my charcoal pants. A black clip-on bow tie with pink
polka dots, black and gold cuff links, and black shoes with white
socks completed my outfit. That was my Rock and Roll outfit and
I wore it often. I felt dressed-up when I wore it in New York City
in the spring of 1956 during our senior class trip. I am certain that
Jayne Mansfield and Orson Bean both thought so when they signed
my program after attending, "Will Success Spoil Rock Hunter" on
Broadway.

I mention my suit, in part, since Wallis also wore it on occasion. He borrowed it once and kept it for a while out at Uncle Joe's
farm. It upset him when I jokingly wondered when I would get it
back. Uncle Joe Pope and his three sisters took Wallis in to live with

them when he was in about the seventh grade. Joe and his sisters were Wallis's great uncle and aunts on his mother's side. None of them had ever married except his Aunt Ellen. She moved back with the others when she lost her husband and daughter. Wallis went to live with them after his father died. Wallis's sister, Janelle, went to live with Aunt Maude who was their mother's sister and who taught school in Fort Pierce, Florida. Uncle Joe's farm was located just off the Statesboro and Savannah Highway past Brooklet, Georgia. It seemed to be an authentic pioneer homestead. It was set among old growth trees and those pines in the woods were of virginal quality. Wallis invited me once or twice to spend a night there. It was an unforgettable experience. His aunts went overboard with food preparation. We had a wonderful supper one evening that featured turkey hash. It was cold weather when we visited and I recall sleeping under several homemade quilts. Wallis carried me out squirrel hunting during the day with his rifle. I killed my first and only squirrel ever. Uncle Joe loved to dear hunt and he had dogs to help.

Wallis was a sophomore and I was a "Rat" during the fall of 1956. I had to wear a "rat cap" along with all the other freshmen. We were never to be caught without our caps on our heads. Wallis told me not to offend any of the sophomores and obey all their commands. If I didn't, "they might take you out to Bird's Pond, throw you in and leave you to walk home," he said. There was considerable hazing of freshmen before "Rat Week" arrived. I heard of one or two students who had indeed had been thrown in and left at Bird's Pond. The final hazing came after dark late one night when the sophomores got us out of bed and led us outside wearing only our underwear and our rat caps. They had prepared a mud bog out behind Sanford Hall and we had to wallow in it while they shot cold water on us from a fireman's hose. They finally took us out and hosed us down and proceeded to parade us around Sweetheart Circle in front of the three girl's dorms. It was cold, and our underwear and rat caps were our only protection. The college administration gave their stamp of approval to this yearly event.

Wallis helped me get a job in the dining hall in order to help meet expenses. He had worked there, but found a better job in the Biology Department as an assistant to Dr. Boole and Dr. Pennington. The dining hall job paid fifty cents an hour. I worked all three meals and still didn't have enough to pay my tuition at the end of the quarter. I arose very early to help "lay bacon" and make orange juice from concentrate at breakfast. At lunch and dinner, I usually served "first meat" unless I was "running roles". The dietician, Mrs. Melton, believed in having hot rolls. Towards my junior and senior year, I was promoted to "line checker" and cashier. I was given a little gadget that I clicked to count the number of students who came through the line each meal. I was expected to know which students were non-residential and collect money from them to pay for their meal. I let one or two of my friends by occasionally without paying. Perhaps I should make restitution and send the school a few dollars.

Wallis really helped me stay in college by introducing me to The Pickett and Hatcher Education Loan Fund. It had been his main source of financial aid. This was a loan fund established by the Nehi Corporation out of Columbus, Georgia. It would lend money at a very low interest and did not have to be repaid until the student was out of school for four months. The loan payment was ten percent of the person's salary who took out the loan. As long as the student remained in school, only the interest had to be paid each year. Three co-signers were required before the loan was granted. My uncle Clarence Fambro and my brother-in-law George Huguley were two knowledgeable signers of my loan, but daddy never knew I signed his name. I was able to continue at Georgia Southern for the remainder of my three years due to this great fund. I owed only fifteen hundred dollars by the time I graduated. I started repaying the loan when I got my first job teaching in Americus. When I entered graduate school at the University of Georgia three years later, I only had to pay the interest on the balance of the loan. I did not pay the loan off until I came to Valdosta State in 1968. It is remarkable how much a college education costs today--and I use the term education loosely. Fifteen hundred dollars is about half the cost for one semester for a non-resident at Valdosta State.

Wallis loved to dance almost as much as I did, but he was a little reserved when it came to "really getting down". He found it hard to "undulate" which is the first prerequisite for "getting it on". We hardly ever missed a "mat dance" (matinee) after supper each Wednesday night in the old gym. This was the era of Elvis and rock and roll. It was about the same as a "Sock Hop" and there were always some of the faculty who came to chaperone. Larger formal dances were often held in the same place on certain Saturday nights during the quarter. The college band ensemble played live music and sometimes Emma Kelly from town played the piano with them. This was before Emma started singing and long before she was inducted into the Georgia Music Hall of Fame.

Wallis had to temporarily drop out of college near the end of that year. He had a problem with his mother. I first learned of it when I walked into his room and noticed that his eyes were red from crying. I asked what was wrong, and he told me about his mother's history of alcoholism and his pressing problem. "My mother has been arrested and put in jail in Savannah for having been habitually arrested on repeated charges. They are going to put her away in the penitentiary unless I do something." He told me he went over to Savannah and talked to his mother. "I had to talk with her through a little hole in the wall," he said. He also went to the judge and pleaded for her release. He promised the judge that he would take her out of Savannah and the state of Georgia if only he would release her to him and not send her to prison for habitual arrests.

The judge granted Wallis's request, and he left college to take his mother Blanche down to Eau Gallie, Florida. The name is pronounced "Oh Galley". It is about an hour east of Orlando. It is now considered part of Melbourne since the city governments merged in 1969. It was near Cape Canaveral Missile Base which was later changed to Cape Kennedy. Wallis found a job at the base as a trajectory film reader. I never knew just what he did. He also got a job washing dishes at night at a popular restaurant on the beach. Due to the boom of new jobs at the base housing was in short supply--especially affordable housing. Wallis was lucky to find a one bedroom upstairs garage apartment. His mother and sister, Janelle, who had come to help, shared the bedroom whereas Wallis slept in the downstairs garage portion that had been fitted with a bed but hardly anything else.

Wallis kept in contact with me by mail during the remainder of the year and encouraged me to get a job at the base during the coming summer. It would be great fun to be together again and I could live with his family. He furnished me with addresses of companies at the base to contact for employment. Our secret was that I would only work for that one summer, but I should tell them that I was to be full time since I had to drop out of college for a while. I forgot the name of the company with which I corresponded and applied for a job. There were numerous companies that had contracts at Cape Canaveral during this post-Sputnik era. That entire area was undergoing a big change with lots of hustle and bustle.

By the end of spring quarter that year, I was all set to come in for an interview for a job in the personnel department of a particular company. The interview was on Monday morning. I was back to Poulan by then and was lucky to find a ride to Eau Gallie with Carlos Branch, who along with his brother-in-law, Buford Dowdy, had banking jobs down there. Carlos came home to Poulan almost every week-end since he had not yet moved his family with him.

I kept my appointment that Monday and had a successful interview. I was to be placed in some area of personnel. The lady told me I should report the following Monday for work. I was real excited the rest of the week as I visited with Wallis and his family.

I rode back to Poulan with Carlos late Friday afternoon to get my clothes and things. I also needed to persuade Troy to let me drive the 1951 maroon Chevy coupe that we owned together. I had to have transportation to go back and forth to the base. He agreed and I drove back down to Eau Gallie that Sunday afternoon. I had never driven that far by myself, but I managed to stay on the right roads.

When I reported for work Monday morning, I was informed that I did not have a job. I was told that a person on a leave of absence came back and was given the job I was promised. That news was sheer devastation. I didn't know what to do and had no funds. Wallis insisted that I make the rounds to almost every company at the base to find a job. I spent the next two weeks doing that, but no job was to be found. I somehow felt that I was being punished for my lying about wanting a full time job when I didn't. The only solution was to get back home and go to work in the cotton mill if I could.

With hardly enough money for gas, I headed back home in the little maroon Chevy. The trip was long and there were no interstates as there now. As I was getting closer to home, I noticed around Adel, Georgia the engine was running hot. I needed oil but didn't have any money to buy any, so I continued on with a very hot motor. As I was going over the new over-head bridge in Poulan that night, the motor stopped and was smoking real bad. I coasted on in to what is known today as "Ed's Truck Stop". This was a little short order and service station owned by Bill McPhaul where Troy worked. The car engine was shot and I took a lot of cussing for burning it up. "Before letting it burn up, you should have stopped at a station and asked for some used motor oil if you didn't have any money," he said. I did make a terrible mistake for not doing better. Somehow Troy got the motor fixed and we had transportation once more.

Sometime later that summer, I got a letter from Wallis asking me to go to California with him and his family. It was decided that he and his mother would drive his sister Janelle out to Fresno where cousin Freida lived and worked. Janelle hoped to find work out there as well. I was real excited at the possibility of such a trip since I had only barely crossed over the Georgia border into Florida and Alabama. I told him I would, and he agreed to come through Poulan and pick me up. We would be driving a 1952 Plymouth that he had bought on credit. I can't remember whether I was working full time in the Poulan mill, but I somehow came up with forty dollars to take me to California and back! I don't suppose I realized how far off California was from Poulan, Georgia, nor did I know how long we would be visiting there. There was no back-up plan in case some need arose. My family didn't even have a telephone back then. We depended mostly on the USP, and in a real emergency, we might call someone in Poulan who we knew had a phone and ask them to deliver a message.

I don't remember the day or the hour we departed from Poulan on our way west, but I must have been as excited as the first time I flew to another country. Back then, going to California was almost the equivalent of going overseas--at least by my reasoning. I have always experienced being "journey proud" before taking a trip and I suspect that I must have been terribly so back then. Wallis said that we intended to drive all the way there without any overnight stops since we had no money for motels. Wallis, Janelle, and I would alternate with the driving both day and night. I didn't pay much attention to the route taken or the highway signs. I was content following the course that Wallis had charted. We must have driven through Alabama and Mississippi during the first night. I remember stopping for a wonderful breakfast somewhere in Arkansas that first morning.

As I am presently attempting to retrace our journey to California, I realize for the first time that we traveled much of our journey on the famous "Route 66." We picked up the route near Oklahoma City and continued with it until we reached the Grand

Canyon. We left it when we went north to Las Vegas. Route 66 is also known as "The Mother Road" first mentioned by John Steinbeck in "Grapes of Wrath." It was on this road that many "Arkies" and "Okies" traveled west during the depression and the dust bowl days in search of work in the California fields. It has also been referred to as "The Main Street of America" as well as "The Will Rogers Highway". Wikipedia credits Bobby Troup with first recording the song "Route 66". We traveled the route before "Get Your Kicks On Route 66" emerged in the entertainment industry. I never realized until now that the eastern origin of the route was Chicago, and it cut somewhat diagonally down through Kansas to Oklahoma and ended in Las Angeles. It was later extended to the west coast. Sadly, much of this famous route doesn't exist any longer except for historical markers. During the Eisenhower years the Interstate Highway System was begun and soon put an end to several old highways as "Route 66" and the "Lincoln Highway."

I wish I had written a journal during the trip, but that seemed unimportant to a college sophomore. A camera would also have been a great tool to help document our trip, but there was no money for such a luxury. As we traveled through Oklahoma, I saw my first oil well. Some, I believe, were on the statehouse grounds. We might have seen a Native American or two as we passed through the state. In checking the internet, there are numerous sites that are devoted to Route 66 . Some specialize in iconic places and unusually famous attractions along the highway. We might have stopped at some of them, but most of our stopping was for gas or restrooms. I remember traveling through northern Texas during the early morning hours before daybreak. I have never been as cold as then and it was in mid-summer.

By the end of the second and third day, I was very tired and suffered from the loss of sleep. Even so, I was excited when we came upon the Painted Desert with the myriad of colors. I had never heard of the Petrified Forest until I saw it the same day. We turned off the main road and took a drive through the place. A prominent sign was placed at the entrance warning tourists that it was illegal to take any petrified wood as souvenirs. I was amazed at the number of logs and large specimens that I saw as well as the abundance of small pieces of wood that were lying around. Surely no one would miss a very tiny piece. Janelle and I both took a small piece and hid it in the blanket on the back seat. Janelle had a much greater conscience than I did and worried that we had stolen something. Just before we exited the park, she threw her piece of petrified wood out the window. She claimed she was making restitution. Janelle had been raised with a great deal of Catholic schooling, and Wallis told me she had thought about becoming a nun after graduation. Aunt Maude might have helped her change her mind. Regardless, as we left the Petrified Forrest, there were numerous souvenir shops selling petrified wood . I learned on the internet that tons of wood are removed from the park each year. We drove on to Winslow, Arizona and stopped for lunch. While in the restaurant, we experienced a severe wind and sand storm. I had never seen sheets of sand move like that. That sand storm would become quite consequential for us after we got to Fresno.

The Grand Canyon was quite a few miles off our main course, but there was no way that we would miss it. We headed from Flagstaff to Williams and then north to reach the canyon. By this time my eyes were heavy and burning, not from the sand storm in Winslow, but from the lack of sleep. Nevertheless, I was eager see one of the wonders of the U.S. I never knew what "grand" meant until I saw the canyon that first time. I didn't realize it would be that vast, cavernous, and awesome. It was indeed a sight to behold. I wonder if I could have appreciated it more had my eyes not been so very tired and burning. We were at the south rim and at the sight of the El Tovar Hotel that was constructed about 1905. Theodore Roosevelt and other dignitaries had slept there. The Hopi Indians were doing a dance near the hotel. I finally got to see a real American Indian dance. I always chose to be the Indian when we played "Cowboys and Indians" as a child. One of the two whippings my daddy gave me was when I pretended to be a real Indian around one of the three wig-whams we built in Jeanette Branch's yard. Ever the actor, I went home, took off my clothes and strapped two pieces of material over my front and rear end. I put a case knife in the belt that held my outfit. I wanted to be authentic as possible and ran back across the road to our Indian village. Jeanette's dad caught a glimpse of my naked rear end as I was doing a dance around the tee-pee. He told me to go put my clothes on. He told my father about the incident a week later, and I got a whipping that bordered on abusive. I never cared for Jeanette's dad after that, and I avoided him like the plague.

I kept the image of the El Tovar Hotel in my mind for many years. I loved and appreciated the rusticity and beauty of the place. I wished that we could have stayed there that night, but the cost would no doubt have been prohibitive. We left the canyon and headed back to Williams. I was able to actually stay at the El Tovar only recently when we visited Janelle and husband Richard in Phoenix. They were kind enough to drive us on a great tour of the area.

After leaving the canyon, we were desperate for a bath and a good night's sleep. Wallis decided we would get a motel room. I believe it must have been in, or near, Williams. It wasn't the El Tovar, but it was the first time I had ever stayed in a motel. I don't remember any of the details, but we all probably crashed immediately after eating and checking into the place. We went to bed with visions of passing through Las Vegas the next day.

The Las Vegas we saw is nothing comparable to what it is today. I have never been back there, but I see pictures of the place with so many mega hotels and casinos. I primarily remember Freemont Street with all the lights and of course the "Golden Nugget". Wallis' '52 Plymouth broke down right on Freemont, and we had to push it around the corner to a garage. The mechanic said we needed a new alternator. While they were repairing the car, we all went into the Golden Nugget Casino. I was amazed at the slot machines all over the place--even in the bathroom. We really had no money to waste, but we had to try our luck. Wallis has always been somewhat of a gambler. He was always deeply religious, but he did like the slots and the race track. His Aunt Maude also liked to gamble too according to him. I recall loosing quite a bit of my meager funds on the slots. Thank goodness a security guard escorted Wallis and me out the door for being under twenty-one years of age. Had he not intervened, I would have gone on to California without a red cent. I might go back to Las Vegas one day and I am certain that if I do, I want to stay right on Freemont at the Golden Nugget.

We headed on to Fresno after leaving Vegas. I can't recall much of anything about the last leg of our journey. I must have been sleeping much of the time before arriving in Fresno at Freida's place. Freida was Aunt Maude's only child. I do not know what type of job she had in Fresno and why she was working so far from home. I believe she must have been Civil Service. She was considerably older than Janelle, Wallis, and me and had not yet married. I am certain she wasn't overly excited to have four adults living with her since she only had an efficiency apartment. There was a sofa bed that was made-up each night. Some of us slept on the floor on the cushions while others slept on the sofa. The apartment was very expensive, Wallis said.

I forget many details of our stay, but shortly after our arrival, something went wrong with Wallis' car. He took it to some mechanic who Wallis's cousin Freida knew. The mechanic said that the motor "got sanded" and it would be a big job to fix it. This happened when we had stopped for lunch in Winslow, Arizona during that terrible sand storm. According to the mechanic we should have known to have the oil changed immediately after the storm. This wasn't good news since there was no money for a repair job. Without question, the car had to be fixed and paid for somehow. We scanned the paper for temporary jobs. Janelle was already looking for full time work which was the reason we went to Fresno in the first place. Wallis said we could get a job working in the fields with migrant workers. I told him I could not do that since I had only one pair of shoes and didn't want to ruin them. Wallis said he could work barefoot and he went to work. I saw an ad in the paper from a dance studio in town. It was either the Arthur Murry or Fred Astair Dance Studio. They needed to hire males as dance instructors. I was naively confident that I could do this job even though I had never had any formal dance training. I had been taught how to do the "Charleston" when I was in high school and participated in the Worth County Centennial. Some guy from New Your City was the show's director and he taught us the "Charleston". My only other asset was that I enjoyed dancing and knew how to do the jitterbug and shag and slow partner dancing came easy for me. I walked quite a long way to the main part of town to have an interview with the studio. I am not sure if they asked me to dance, but they told me to come back the next day to begin working. When I asked about pay, they said I would be paid after two weeks. That wasn't good news since we expected to leave Fresno by then, so I didn't return to the studio. I actually believe the whole thing was a scam. I believe they were attempting to entice men to come into the studio to work as dance partners for older women who were paying for the program. Who knows? Had I have taken that job, perhaps some wealthy mature lady might have left me a fortune and changed my entire life.

Our extended stay in Fresno gave us a lot of free time--especially me, since I was "too good" to work in the fields with Wallis. When Wallis wasn't working, he and I walked a good distance to the Fresno Zoo. We did this a few times and it was free entertainment. One day when we were standing by the Chimp cage at the zoo, a male worker handed the baby chimp a banana. The daddy chimp took the banana away from the baby and started to eat it. The quick and talented mother chimp immediately snatched the banana from the daddy and returned it to the baby. In order to distract and pacify the daddy, she turned herself upside down and put her bottom end in his face. She also manipulated his "manhood"at the same time. Wallis and I screamed with laughter as well as did the two Black females who were observing beside us.

Our other form of entertainment was playing Hearts in the apartment. We really got to know that game. We were still in Fresno on July the fourth and Freida was off that day. She decided she would drive us over to San Francisco. After getting on the highway, she thought otherwise since there was too much traffic. Instead, she decided to take us to see the Yosemite National Park. I had never seen real mountains and such natural beauty as we witnessed riding through that park. I couldn't believe it when we rode through a tunnel made through a giant sequoia tree. It was most probably the Wawona Tunnel Tree and the same as the one I remembered seeing a picture of in my elementary school geography book. I learned from the internet that this tree finally fell in the winter of l968-69. Among the most spectacular and truly awesome vistas was observing the several waterfalls as the Yosemite Falls and Bridal Veil Falls. El Capitan and Half Dome Mountains were among the many peaks we observed as we rode though the valley. I had no camera, but I did buy a few picture post cards to help document our visit. Some of these cards are presently up in the attic in my box of keepsakes. I sent some to Mama back in Poulan. One of the most memorable events at Yosemite was the ride back down from the highest point. As our car continuously wound downward I was overcome with motion sickness and being in the back seat didn't help. Finally, we had to stop and let me out so that I wouldn't vomit in the car. In retrospect, I feel the trip through the park was well worth the car sickness and I would do it all over again if necessary.

I don't recall when Wallis' car got repaired and just when we started back to Georgia. It wasn't too long after our tour of Yosemite. Likewise, I am not sure how much the repair job cost. I only regret now that I had no funds to help. I wasn't nearly as resourceful as Wallis has always been. Wallis was always a bundle of energy and very creative when the need arose. I now have a great deal of guilt for not taking off my precious shoes and going out into the fields with the migrant workers and pulling my weight with him. Wallis, his mother, and I left Fresno in the repaired '52 Plymouth. Wallis decided we would take a southern route back home. The first thing I remember on our journey home was going through Phoenix, Arizona and how terribly hot it was in the car. Wallis said we should stop and go to a movie in order to cool off in the air conditioned theater. I can't remember the name of the movie, but I believe it was a double feature. Wallis cooled off quickly and was too restless to stay for the end of the movie. We were cooler for a while.

I always thought our car broke down as we passed over the Coolidge Dam and we coasted into Deming, New Mexico. In looking at the map, I realize this was incorrect since the dam is near Globe, Arizona which is quite a distance west of Deming. I also remember going to El Paso, Texas and Juarez, Mexico before the car broke down and these are a good distance south-east of Deming. Suffice it to say, our car broke down somewhere in south-eastern New Mexico at about two o'clock a.m. and we coasted into a service station that was closed for the night. We tried to sleep but kept worrying about what we were going to do since we had no money. Being inventive again, Wallis even talked about going to the Salvation Army and asking for help. When the service station opened the next morning, the owner told us that the car had slung a rod. That was devastating news. There was no money and if we had, it would take a long time to repair the car. What were we to do? The man offered Wallis twenty-five dollars for the car. Wallis agreed, but I thought it terrible since he still owed two hundred and fifty dollars on it; plus, he had spent lots of money on the motor repair in Fresno, he had new tires, a new alternator, and it was almost full of gas.

Wallis decided that we should buy a bus ticket for his mother and send her back to Fresno. He told me to try to get some money somehow so we could pay partial bus fare back to Georgia.

His mother went on back to Freida's and Janell's. At Wallis's suggestion, I called my sister in Phenix City, Alabama and asked her if she could wire me twenty dollars to Dallas, Texas by Western Union. Wallis had enough money for our bus tickets there. Mary Nell didn't have any money, but she agreed to try to borrow some.

We got off the bus in Dallas and walked to the Western Union. Thankfully, she had sent the twenty dollars, but we got a few dollars less due to the transaction fee they charged. I found out later that she had borrowed the money from a former neighbor, Mrs. Sink, when Mary Nell lived by her on Front Avenue in Columbus, Georgia. Mrs. Sink was a real character. She was the classic obsessive-compulsive personality. Every morning found her with her house broom in hand sweeping the leaves from her front yard. She wore a bobbed haircut and a sleeveless dress that allowed her bra strap to worry her a bit as she swept. She wore thick glasses that enabled her to pick up a leaf as soon as it fell. In later years, she had all the trees in her front yard removed and placed gravel in the concrete bordered squares on each side of her walk where the trees had been. Mary Nell never let me forget the fact that I borrowed twenty dollars from her. I only hope and pray that she repaid Mrs. Sink.

We were able to buy a bus ticket as far as Shreveport, Louisiana. We got off there and began hitch-hiking for a while to save what little money we had. We were fortunate to get several rides that carried us nearer to Georgia. I noticed trees like those at home for the first time around Shreveport. I enjoyed the countryside and talking with those who gave us a ride such as the farmer who drove us several miles in his pick-up. At some point, we got back on the same bus and rode into Montgomery. We were lucky enough with our hitch-hiking to stay ahead of the same bus we got off of in Shreveport. We rode a city bus that morning from the Montgomery bus station out to the edge of town where we hitched-hiked into Phenix City, Alabama. I believe Mary Nell picked us up there and we went to her house. Wallis didn't tarry too long, and we took him to the edge of town so he could hitch a ride on to Statesboro.

I might have stayed overnight with Mary Nell, but I believe I had her drop me off later that afternoon on the south end of Columbus Highway 82, so I could hitch my way on home. My first ride was with a nice family that took me as far as Richland. I somehow got to Albany where an older man who said he was going to Tifton picked me up. I was glad when he dropped me off in Poulan in front of Mr. Moore's grocery store. I was becoming a little uncomfortable with his conversation and suggestions.

Poulan wasn't California, or the many towns between, but it was home, and as Dorothy said, "There is no place like home". I was very glad to lie down on my old feather bed, even in hot weather, and taste Mama's cooking again. I am also very grateful to have met Wallis DeWitt, who, with his family, became a big part of my extended family.

*P.S. I began my second year at Georgia Southern the following fall. Although details are lacking, Wallis returned to college either in the fall or winter quarter of that year. We suffered through a Physics class together among other things. He, nor I, could ever do math related things. I remember him jumping on my dorm bed when my roommate, Ray Wilson, a math major, said he could help explain a physics problem. Wallis went wild as he jumped up and down on my bed while saying, "God Himself doesn't understand it and he doesn't intend for me to understand it"!*

*His mother, Janell and Freida left Fresno and returned to Florida a few weeks after we left. His mother, at some point, went back to Savannah and had a short remarriage before she was found dead. The death was most probably alcohol induced. Wallis finished College and found work at Johns Hopkins Hospital doing Biological Research. He married Jeanette Peavy in the fall of 1960. He got an M.S. in Bacteriology at the University of Georgia and a Masters of Public Health at Tulane in New Orleans. He had a long and interesting career at CDC in Atlanta prior to retiring after about forty years. He never lost his love of travel and he developed many friends*